THE BEST OF
JENNY'S KITCHEN

COOKING NATURALLY WITH VEGETABLES

THE BEST OF
JENNY'S KITCHEN

JENNIFER RAYMOND

AVON
PUBLISHERS OF BARD, CAMELOT, DISCUS AND FLARE BOOKS

AVON BOOKS
A division of
The Hearst Corporation
959 Eighth Avenue
New York, New York 10019

Cover illustration by Mary Sherman
Book design by Joyce Kubat

First Avon Printing, June, 1982

Library of Congress Cataloging in Publication Data:

Raymond, Jennifer.
   The best of Jenny's kitchen.

   Includes index.
   1. Cookery (Vegetables)   2. Cookery (Natural foods)
I. Title.
TX801.R385   1982   641.6'5   81-70584
ISBN 0-380-58461-1   AACR2

Printed in the U.S.A.

DON 10 9 8 7 6 5 4 3 2 1

Dedicated to a more equitable
distribution of the world's resources,
and to those deeply concerned persons
whose altered lifestyles reflect
true caring and conservation

Special thanks to all the friends who insisted that this book be compiled and then encouraged and assisted in the process; my mother, Lois Jean, for her enthusiasm and genuine interest—she was my first student; my husband, Bruce, for his patience and encouragement throughout; and all my students, for their interest, and for the knowledge and recipes they have shared.

PREFACE

Jenny's Kitchen—a special place...

Certainly, my kitchen is adequate. It's sunny and neatly laid out.

But Jenny's kitchen is more. Hers has a pulse...a fragrant something that is always stirring or rising or steaming...in Jenny's kitchen.

My kitchen is always clean and proper, everything in place.

Hers is a merry blur. Lining the plate rail, colorful jars hold beans and seeds and mysterious kernels. A fire is on the hearth. Shiny bowls and sturdy tools adorn the shelves, and on the stove, the teakettle is always at the ready.

So, pull up a chair and clear a place among the lists and plans there on the table. Relax awhile, and feel the life in Jenny's kitchen.

LOIS JEAN RAYMOND

INTRODUCTION

In addition to presenting an exciting collage of creative vegetarian dishes, this book has three objectives:

1. To answer the inevitable query, "What do vegetarians eat?"
2. To provide specific and practical suggestions for dietary changes that will have an impact on the problems of inequity in a world of shrinking resources.
3. To offer motivation for healthier eating habits.

Jenny asks, What is the matter with genuine cooking? It is a beautiful and satisfying art form, in danger of being lost to the national passion for flashy, prefabricated, so-called convenience foods.

Genuine cooking is steadily being replaced by clever combining of manufactured ingredients, and many cookbooks are no longer really *cookbooks*, but simply combining guides. Beware of the recipe that begins with a can of mushroom soup or ends with a squirt of aerosol topping.

The recipes that follow are not contrived. They are not fast, but neither are they needlessly tedious. All of them have been successfully prepared within the time frame of a classroom. All of them use whole, unprocessed ingredients.

Take time to discover the joy of cooking. There is real pleasure and deep satisfaction in proper handling and careful preparation of fresh, beautiful foods from the earth.

CONTENTS

Nutrition

PROTEIN

The first thing most people ask me when they find out I'm a vegetarian is, "How do you get enough protein?" Even folks who have no other concerns about the adequacy of their diets worry about getting enough protein.

There are three things you should know about protein.

First, the majority of Americans eat more protein than they actually need—two to three times as much, in fact. It used to be thought that extra protein couldn't hurt you, but now we're learning otherwise. Excess protein, which is not burned for energy, is converted to fat. In addition, a high protein intake may be related to high blood pressure, kidney disease, and osteoporosis, or loss of calcium from the bones.

Second, you should know how much protein you actually need. This can be determined by looking at the chart on page 6, or by multiplying your ideal body weight (the amount you should weigh) by .37 grams. This will tell you how many grams of protein you need each day. The average protein requirement for an adult is 50 grams per day.

Finally, you should know which foods to eat in order to meet your daily protein requirement. A vegetarian diet contains five major food groups. These are:

1. Dairy products—milk, cheese, yogurt, eggs
2. Legumes—beans and peas (also peanuts)
3. Grains—rice, wheat, corn, millet, rye, etc. (includes potatoes)
4. Nuts and seeds—sunflowers seeds, walnuts, sesame seeds, etc.
5. Vegetables and fruits

By combining foods from one group with foods of certain other groups, you can get high-quality, or complete, protein. The best food-group combinations are:

Dairy products with grains:
   Cereal with milk
   Bread with cheese
   Macaroni and cheese
   Scalloped potatoes
   Crackers with cheese
   Cream soups and bread
   Yogurt shake with toast
   Pizza (crust and cheese)
   Baked goods made with milk
   Rice casserole with cheese
   Pasta with cheese (lasagna)
   Rice or bread pudding

Complete-protein yields of some dairy-grain combinations are:

1 cup milk	plus ¾ cup rice		yields 17 grams	
¼ cup grated cheese	" ¾ cup rice	"	17	"
⅓ cup milk	" 2 slices bread	"	9	"
1 oz. cheese	" 2 slices bread	"	9	"
1 oz. cheese	" 1½ cups bulgur	"	28	"
½ cup milk	" 1 cup whole-wheat flour	"	14	"
1 cup milk	" 1 potato	"	9	"
⅓ cup grated cheese	" 1 potato	"	9	"

Legumes with grains:
  Tofu with rice
  Beans and rice
  Beans and tortillas
  Beans and cornmeal
  Lentil soup and bread
  Peanut butter sandwich
  Lentils and rice (Mjeddrah)
  Baked goods with soy flour
  Split pea soup with biscuits

Complete-protein yields:

½ cup beans	plus	1⅓ cups rice	yields	30	grams
¼ cup soybeans	″	2½ cups rice	″	37	″
3 oz. tofu	″	1 cup rice	″	37	″
¼ cup soy flour	″	1 cup wheat flour	″	16	″
¼ cup beans	″	1 cup cornmeal	″	14	″
¼ cup beans	″	6 tortillas	″	14	″
½ cup beans	″	2½ cups bulgur	″	46	″

fig. 1

4

Legumes with nuts and seeds:
    Falafel
    Tofu with sesame seeds
    Granola made with soy flour and sesame seeds
    Salad made with garbanzos and sunflower seeds

Complete-protein yields:

⅓ cup beans	plus	½ cup sesame seed	yields	19	grams
⅓ cups beans	"	¼ cup tahini	"	19	"
¾ cup peanuts	"	1 cup sunflower seed	"	55	"
½ cup peanut butter	"	1 cup sunflower seed	"	55	"

All complementary proportions refer to cooked foods when applicable.

Other good protein combinations include rice with sesame seeds, beans with milk or cheese, and nuts or seeds with milk or cheese.

If you eat a reasonable amount of any of the above combinations, you can be certain of meeting your daily protein requirement.

If you are still concerned, the chart on page 32 lists the protein per serving for each recipe. Using this chart, you can calculate your daily protein intake.

RECOMMENDED DAILY
PROTEIN REQUIREMENT

	Age	Weight	Height	Protein
Infants	0–½	14 lb.	24 in.	1g/lb.
	½–1	20	28	.9g/lb.
Children	1–3	28	34	23g
	4–6	44	44	30g
	7–10	66	54	36g
Adolescents				
Girls	11–14	97	62	44g
	15–18	119	65	48g
	19–22	128	65	46g
Boys	11–14	97	63	44g
	15–18	134	69	54g
	19–22	147	69	54g
Adults				
Women	23–50	128	65	46g
	51+	128	65	46g
Men	23–50	154	69	56g
	51+	154	69	56g
Pregnant				30g+
Lactating				40g+

Source: Food and Nutrition Board, National Research Council, 1974.

CARBOHYDRATES

For some time, carbohydrates have borne an undeserved reputation as starchy foods with little value and lots of calories. Many people tend to think of carbohydrates only as "fillers" in their diets, the first thing to eliminate when they need to lose weight.

Contrary to this notion is the increasing realization among nutritionists of the importance of carbohydrates in the diet. They are the body's most perfect source of energy, the only nutrient which can be burned for energy with no harmful by-products. Carbohydrates provide an excellent source of B vitamins. They provide fiber, or bulk, in the diet, which is necessary for proper elimination, and may be beneficial in preventing hemorrhoids, diverticulosis, cancer of the colon, and heart disease.

However, a distinction must be made between refined and unrefined carbohydrates. *Refined* carbohydrates are foods such as white sugar, white flour, potato chips, candy, etc., which have had most of the nutrients removed or destroyed in processing. They offer little nutrition, lots of empty calories, and are effective fat-makers and constipators. *Refined carbohydrates* should be avoided.

Unrefined, or complex, carbohydrates include fresh fruits and vegetables, whole grains, and legumes. According to most nutrition authorities, Americans need to *increase* consumption of these foods, while *decreasing* use of refined carbohydrates, fats, and protein.

Practically, this means using whole-grain breads and cereals, eating more fresh fruits and vegetables, and decreasing animal sources of protein in the diet. If this is a change for you and your family, try making it gradually: Substitute whole-wheat flour for half the white flour (or unbleached flour) you are now using. Try incorporating brown rice into a casserole before you serve it plain. Begin decreasing the amount of sweetener in desserts by a half

7

or quarter, or serve fresh fruit, topped with yogurt and granola, instead.

Other suggestions:

Begin using cereals that are made with whole grains. If these are too different, try mixing them with old familiar favorites.

Begin reading labels, and avoid breakfast cereals that list sugar (or honey, corn syrup, or dextrose) as a first ingredient. Also eliminate cereals that contain more than one kind of sugar, as these usually contain more sugar than anything else.

Use fresh fruit instead of canned, or can your own without sugar. Commercially canned fruit usually contains a high percentage of sugar.

Use fresh vegetables or those frozen without sauce. Many canned vegetables have added sugar, as do many that are frozen with sauce. Read the labels.

Have apple slices (or other cut-up fruits and vegetables) ready as an after-school snack. Dried fruits and nuts are also good snacks.

Eliminate *all* soft drinks. Try unsweetened fruit juices, and for a bit of bubbly, try mixing them with mineral water.

It has been known for some time that an excess of dietary fat is an effective means of producing body fat. An increasing volume of scientific evidence also indicates a direct relationship between high-fat diets and many common degenerative diseases: obesity, heart disease, stroke, gallstones, diabetes, certain cancers, and even arthritis.

In spite of this evidence, Americans consume more than 40 percent of their calories in the form of fat. About a third of this is undisguised—butter, margarine, dips and dressings—but the other two-thirds is hidden in meat, milk, pastries, and sauces.

Many people are aware of the cholesterol theory of heart disease, and have made efforts to decrease consumption of cholesterol and saturated fats, often by increasing their intake of unsaturated fats. Recent research, however, has shown that *unsaturated* fats may also be linked with heart disease, and certain types of cancer are more prevalent in individuals who use large amounts of unsaturated fats. In view of this evidence, most nutrition authorities recommend a decreased consumption of all fats—unsaturated as well as saturated.

In developing the recipes for this book, I have attempted to use as little fat as possible, while keeping the end product acceptable to the average person's taste. You will notice that in recipes requiring a solid shortening, I have used butter. This is because butter is a minimally processed, relatively unadulterated food, whereas margarine and vegetable shortening are highly processed and contain numerous additives. However, if you are concerned about your cholesterol intake, margarine or shortening should be substituted for the butter.

PREGNANCY AND LACTATION

The primary thing to remember during pregnancy and lactation is that you are eating for two, and that what you eat will affect your baby as well as yourself. During this time, your need for all essential nutrients increases, and you will be in the best position if you are well nourished *before* you become pregnant.

PREGNANCY

While you are pregnant, the baby gets priority for most nutrients. This means that if a particular nutrient is in short supply in the mother's diet, the mother will experience deficiency symptoms first.

Because you need greater amounts of all nutrients, and because many women experience nausea during the first months of pregnancy (and thus eat less), it is of utmost importance that you get the most from the food you eat. This means *cutting out empty junk foods*—foods that offer little more than calories and chemicals. (This is not to say that calories are bad; it is important that your calorie needs be met each day, or your body will begin to burn much-needed protein for energy. However, food should provide other nutrients as well as calories.)

The amount of weight gained during pregnancy varies according to individual differences. Generally, 25 to 30 pounds is accepted as reasonable weight gain. By the way, if you are overweight, pregnancy is *not* the time to diet. Both you and your baby need adequate nutrients, and these will not be supplied on a reducing diet.

A few nutrients that are especially important are:

Protein—Critical to the baby for normal growth and development, as well as to the mother for mainte-nance of her own health. It was formerly believed that

10

an increase in protein intake was essential only toward the end of pregnancy. However, adequate protein seems to protect against toxemia, and an increase in protein of 30 grams per day throughout pregnancy is now recommended.

One good way to get this additional protein is by drinking 1 quart (4 cups) of low-fat or skim milk per day, or eating 1 cup of low-fat cottage cheese. Besides supplying protein, milk also supplies calcium.

Generally, supplements such as protein powder or tablets are not recommended as a good source of protein, since they are refined foods which are expensive and usually lack other important nutrients.

Calcium—Necessary for formation of bones and teeth in the fetus. Unknown to many people is the fact that adult (permanent) teeth begin to form in the womb. This means that the mother's intake of calcium during pregnancy is critical for the child's permanent teeth. Milk is a good source of calcium, as is tofu.

Iron—Commonly found to be deficient in pregnant women. Insufficient iron causes anemia in the baby as well as in the mother. If the mother gets adequate iron during pregnancy, the baby will be born with a good reserve of iron, to last it through the first six months or so of life when the diet (milk) is low in iron. One excellent source of iron is prune juice (1 cup = 10.5mg); also legumes, grains, and leafy greens.

Vitamin D—A generous supply of this vitamin assures good absorption and utilization of calcium and phosphorus by the fetus. Thus, it is important for the formation of strong teeth and bones. The best sources are sunlight, *fortified* milk, and supplements.

Folacin—This vitamin is essential for proper cell

11

formation and reproduction. One of the most commonly marginal vitamins in the average American diet, this B-complex vitamin is often deficient in pregnant women, showing up as anemia. Best sources are spinach, romaine lettuce, legumes, orange juice, and brewer's yeast.

Vitamin B-12—Essential for proper cell division; may be deficient in women who eat a totally vegetarian diet, that is, use no dairy products. Sources include dairy products, B-12–enriched nutritional yeasts, and supplements (there are a number of nonanimal B-12 supplements available).

NUTRIENT REQUIREMENTS OF NONPREGNANT, PREGNANT, AND LACTATING WOMEN

Nutrient	Nonpregnant Women	Pregnant	Lactating
Calories	2,100	2,300	3,100
Protein	46g	76g	86g
Calcium	800mg	1,200mg	1,200mg
Iron	15mg	20mg	20mg
Vitamin A	5,000 IU	6,000 IU	8,000 IU
Vitamin C	45mg	100mg	100mg
Vitamin D	—	400 IU	400 IU
Folacin	400mg	800mg	600mg
Vitamin B-12	3mg	4mg	4mg

To satisfy the requirements shown in the chart on page 12, the diet of a pregnant or lactating woman should include each day:

Milk — 1 quart low-fat or nonfat

Eggs — not essential, but 1 to 2 eggs per day provide an excellent source of protein

Legumes — 1 large or 2 small servings

Grains — 2 large or 4 small servings, including whole-grain cereal or bread

Vegetables* — 2 or more large servings; at least 1 serving should be dark leafy greens.

Fruits* — 2 or more servings

Brewer's yeast — an excellent supplement to the diet which provides a rich source of several B vitamins, as well as protein, iron, calcium, phosphorus, and potassium. There are a number of different varieties, all with similar nutrients. Some, however, taste significantly better than others. One of these is called Nutritional Yeast (acchoaomyces cerevisiae) and is available in most health food stores.

As far as the need for meat during pregnancy is concerned, Victor Sussman, in his book *The Vegetarian Alternative* (see page 174), states:

> Don't believe anyone who says you must eat meat or fish in order to produce a healthy baby; you need good nutrition, not meat. And neither you nor your baby needs the hormones, pesti-

*Fruits and vegetables are important not only for the nutrients they supply, but also because they help prevent constipation, often a problem experienced by pregnant women.

cides, additives, and adulterants commonly found in much commercially available flesh foods and overprocessed foods. The ultimate effects of toxic residues on fetal and genetic health are still unknown. (You'd be wise, in addition, to give up smoking, drinking, prolonged fasting, and *all* drug use—at least during your pregnancy.)

LACTATION

Nutritive needs increase even more during lactation than during pregnancy. The need for calories, protein, and vitamin A, in particular, increase during this time (see chart on page 12).

Also, a plentiful intake of fluids is important to replace that lost in milk. The recommended amount is 2 to 3 quarts per day.

It should be remembered that the vitamin content of the milk, especially water-soluble vitamins (the B complex and vitamin C), is dependent, at least in part, on the vitamin intake of the mother. If her diet is inadequate, the baby's will almost certainly be lacking.

If you wish to be absolutely certain that you are meeting your (and your baby's) vitamin and mineral requirements, you might consider taking a vitamin-mineral supplement (multiple vitamin) daily. Try to find one that does not contain sugar, artificial flavors, or artificial colors.

There are a number of other substances (besides nutrients) which are passed from the mother to the baby. These include alcohol, drugs—both prescription as well as street varieties—artificial sweeteners, and other toxins in foods. Most authorities recommend avoiding as many of these substances as possible throughout your pregnancy and as long as you are nursing your baby.

In contemplating a vegetarian diet for a dog or cat, the following should be considered:

Dogs and cats are carnivorous by design; thus, a vegetarian diet requires *thorough* planning. Their nutritional requirements are fairly demanding, and a hit-or-miss approach, though it may work for you, is not enough for them.

Dogs need 25 percent more protein per pound than humans, and cats need twice as much protein as dogs. These needs are ten times higher in pregnant and lactating animals, and also for puppies and kittens.

Although meat is an excellent source of protein, it can be replaced by other high-protein foods, such as milk, eggs, cheese, whey, and tofu.

CATS

Cats need a direct source of vitamin A (retinol), as their bodies cannot convert carotene to A. The best vegetarian sources are eggs, cheese, or a vitamin A supplement.

Cats also need niacin, which can be obtained from brewer's yeast, eggs, wheat germ, grains, kelp, and peanuts.

Cats require the amino acid taurine since their bodies cannot synthesize it as ours can. Lack of this amino acid may cause retinal atrophy and eventual blindness.

Cats need a direct source of the essential fatty acids, linolenic and arachadonic. The recommended source is 1 Tbsp. of fish oil per week (no more or you'll have problems with vitamin D toxicity).

DOGS

Dogs need 1 Tbsp. of vegetable oil (safflower, soy, corn, peanut, olive) per day to get the essential fatty acids.

RECIPES

The following recipe is from the book *Laurel's Kitchen* (see page 173) and has, according to the authors, sustained two vegetarian dogs quite satisfactorily for five years.

2 Tbsp. oil
1 cooked egg
2 cups cooked vegetables,
    blended or mashed
1 Tbsp. brewer's yeast
1 cup milk
bread ends and leftover
    cooked cereals and beans

Mix together and serve with love and enthusiasm.

LEGUMES AND GRAINS

The legumes, which include beans, lentils, dried peas, and peanuts, provide an excellent source of protein for the vegetarian diet, especially when combined with grains. In addition, legumes supply calcium, iron, certain B vitamins, fiber, and several other vitamins and minerals.

Legumes should always be washed thoroughly, as they are often quite dusty. Place them in a pot with 3 cups of water for each cup of legume used. Most recipes call for overnight soaking before cooking, and although this is not absolutely necessary, it does cut the cooking time by about a third. A quick way of soaking beans is to put them in a pot with the proper amount of water and bring them to a boil. Allow them to simmer for 2 minutes, then turn off the heat, cover tightly, and let them stand for 1 hour.

To cook legumes, bring them to a boil, then reduce heat and allow them to simmer, covered, for the amount of time specified in the chart on page 19. Check to make sure there is adequate water as they cook.

My favorite way of cooking dried beans is in a crock pot. This eliminates the problem of sticking and burning, and takes no longer than stove-top cooking if you begin with boiling water and set the temperature on high. I generally use a bit less water (about a ¼ less) when cooking in a crock pot. Another advantage of cooking in a crock pot is that all the ingredients in a recipe can be added, uncooked, when you begin cooking the beans. The only exceptions are tomatoes, vinegar, and other acid foods, which will prevent the beans from softening, and should be added at the end of the cooking time.

A pressure cooker may also be used for cooking legumes, although you should be careful not to fill it more than ⅓ full (including water), and make sure the vent does not become clogged; this is especially possible with split peas and soy beans. Add 1 Tbsp. of oil for each cup of cup of beans to prevent foaming. Cooking time for lentils and split peas is 15 minutes; for garbanzos and soybeans, 40 minutes; and for most other beans, about 30 minutes.

GRAINS

When choosing grains, it is best to use those that have been refined as little as possible. For example, use whole-wheat flour rather than white or unbleached, and use regular (old-fashioned) oats rather than the instant varieties.

The reasons for using whole grains are numerous. To begin with, whole grains contain bran or fiber, an indigestible substance which adds bulk to the diet and is necessary for proper elimination. Fiber has the added advantage of being quite filling, and decreasing calorie intake; thus, increasing fiber in the diet (through the use of whole foods) is a safe and effective way of losing excess weight.

Whole grains contain the germ portion of the seed, which supplies vitamin E as well as the essential fatty acid, linoleic acid.

Whole grains are better sources of most vitamins and minerals than refined grains. For example, when wheat is refined, 26 vitamins and minerals are lost or significantly decreased. These include B vitamins, vitamin E, calcium, phosphorus, and potassium, just to name a few. Only four nutrients—thiamin, riboflavin, niacin, and iron—are replaced in "enriched" products.

The chart on page 19 shows proportions, cooking times, and yields of several common legumes and grains.

BEAN AND GRAIN COOKING CHART

Variety (1 cup dry measure)	Amount of water (cups)	Cooking time (hours)	Yield (cups)
BEANS:			
black beans	3	1½	2¼
black-eyed peas	3	1	2
garbanzos	4	3	2½
great northerns	3½	2	2
kidney beans	3	1½	2
lentils	3	1	2¼
lima beans	2	1½	1½
navy beans	3	1½	2
pinto beans	3	2½	2¼
red beans	3	3	2
soybeans	4	3	2½
soy grits	2	20 min.	2
split peas	3	1¼	2½
GRAINS:			
barley	3	1¼	3½
brown rice	2	1	3
buckwheat (kasha)	2	14 min.	2½
bulgur	2	20 min.	2½
cracked wheat	2	25 min.	2½
millet	3	45 min.	3½
polenta (coarse cornmeal)	4	25 min.	3
whole-wheat berries	3	2	2½

It is probably no surprise to hear that Americans eat too much sugar; but did you know that the average American eats approximately ⅓ of a pound of sugar per day? If you're excluding yourself from that statistic, think again, because much of the sugar we eat each day is hidden in foods where we least suspect it. One popular coffee-cream substitute, for example, is 65 percent sugar, many breakfast cereals are over half sugar, and catsup is about 30 percent sugar. These are just a few examples. Most commercially prepared foods contain sugar, and the best way to know if this is true of a particular food is to read the label. You should also check for corn syrup, malt, dextrose, and all other forms of sugar.

Sugar overconsumption is known to be related to obesity and dental decay, and suspected of being linked to diabetes, hyperactivity in children, and heart disease. All forms of sugar have been indicted. Some writers would lead you to believe that certain sweeteners—honey, molasses, "raw" or brown sugar—are different from white sugar. The truth is that these sweeteners all have the negative effects of white sugar. Some, however, have a few redeeming features. Here are the facts:

White sugar—No nutritional value; depletes the body's stores of B vitamins; crowds out more nutritious foods in the diet (such as fresh fruit).

Brown sugar—Simply white sugar with a small amount of molasses added to it; same negative effects as white sugar.

"Raw" sugar—Illegal in the United States, supposedly because it is unsanitary. Sugar sold as raw (including

turbinado) is white sugar with molasses or other coloring added to it (and a high price tag!).

Fructose—Publicized as a "natural" sweetener derived from fresh fruit, and a healthful alternative to refined sugar. This is ironic, as fructose is actually more highly refined than white sugar, and although it is found in fresh fruits, commercially it is derived from corn syrup or sucrose (white sugar!). Fructose does not contain any more nutrients than white sugar, and although claims have been made that it does not cause the drastic fluctuations in blood sugar caused by white sugar, additional research is needed to confirm this. The one known benefit of fructose is that it does taste sweeter than sugar, when used in *cold* foods and drinks, so less can be used. In cooked and hot foods, however, it has about the same sweetening ability as white sugar. Furthermore, as it is currently sold in health food stores, fructose is significantly more expensive than white sugar. Better get your fructose from fruit!

Honey—Has negligible amounts of a few trace minerals, including chromium, which is necessary for the proper metabolism of sugar; may be worse for teeth than white sugar, as it is stickier. One advantage of honey: it tastes sweeter than sugar, so you can use less—about half as much.

Molasses—Long hailed as the "healthful" sweetener, molasses is actually on a nutritional par with honey. It provides little nutritional benefit. One exception is blackstrap molasses, which provides some calcium, iron, and potassium. Blackstrap is rather strong-tasting and not particularly sweet, so use it sparingly until you develop a taste for it.

Maple syrup—Contains some iron, calcium, and potassium; however, it has also been found to contain residues of formaldehyde if produced in the United States (added during the extraction process), and lead (found in both U.S. and Canadian samples).

Date sugar—The only sugar that provides significant food value, date sugar is simply dried dates which have been finely ground. High in iron and potassium, date sugar also supplies B vitamins and protein. It is not as sweet in taste as "real" sugar, and has some tendency to make baked products heavy.

SALT AND SODIUM

Excess sodium in the diet is known to be related to high blood pressure and heart disease. The most abundant source of sodium in our diets is salt—salt added during processing or cooking, and salt added during eating. Sodium is also contained in baking powder, baking soda, monosodium glutamate (MSG), and soy sauce.

Many people mistakenly believe that soy sauce is an acceptable salt alternative, that it is significantly lower in sodium than salt. This is only partly true. A given amount of soy sauce does contain less sodium than an equal amount of salt. However, most people use a lot more soy sauce than salt, making the amount of sodium consumed equal to, or greater than, the amount they consume by eating salt. The point is, if you use soy sauce, use it sparingly. Also, the naturally fermented variety, tamari soy, is preferable to the more commercial varieties, as it does not have artificial color added to it.

There has also been a lot of misinformation about sea salt. Although it contains very small amounts of certain minerals, and *slightly* less sodium than regular salt, it is still salt, and should be respected as such.

The desire for salt is a learned taste. It can be unlearned by gradually decreasing the amount of salt you use in cooking and at the table. In this book, I have attempted to use as little salt as possible while keeping the recipes palatable for the average person's taste. If a recipe seems too salty for you, decrease the amount, or better yet, eliminate it altogether. If you like as much salt as is called for, or perhaps more, begin retraining yourself by using slightly less each time you prepare the recipe. You'll find that, in time, your tastes *will* change, and you'll feel better and be healthier for it.

Baking powder and baking soda both contain sodium and should be used in moderation. Whenever possible, bake a yeast-raised bread rather than a quick bread. When you do use baking powder or soda, experiment with using less than the recipe calls for. Often this can be done without any noticeable difference in the baked product.

Incidentally, many brands of baking powder also contain aluminum and you should check the label for this. Non-aluminum baking powder can be purchased in many health food stores, or you can make your own using the recipe on page 165.

Menu Planning

MENU IDEAS

When planning a menu, pick foods with complementary proteins: dairy and grains; legumes and grains; legumes and nuts/seeds. Also, pick foods with a variety of colors and textures. Besides making a meal appetizing, this usually ensures a variety of nutrients as well.

SAMPLE MENUS:

Vegetable Quiche
French Vegetable Salad
Apple Bran Muffins

Refried Beans II
Cheese Enchiladas
Spanish Rice

Vegetable Curry
Curried Rice
Dal
Cucumber or Banana Raita

Moussaka
Antipasto
Banana Date Pie

Lentil Soup
Vegieburgers
Cucumber Salad

Mjeddrah with Salad
Sesame Sauce on
   Asparagus
Banana Bread

Lasagna
Spinach Salad with Creamy
   Herb Dressing
Hot Herb Bread
Fresh Fruit

Chili Beans
Mexican Rice Bread
Mexican Salad Bowl
Frozen Yogurt

Vegetables and Tofu
Chinese Fried Rice
Spinach Salad with Orange
   Sesame Dressing

Stuffed Chard Leaves
Spicy Carrot Soup
Salad with Basic Vinaigrette
   Dressing

Falafel
Brown Rice Salad
Banana Bonbons

Moussaka
Greek Salad
Banana Date Pie

Zucchini Casserole
Brown Rice Salad
Peanut-Raisin Cookies

Neat Loaf
Green Vegetable Soup
Antipasto

Basic Cheese Soufflé
Tomato Soup
Avocado-Stuffed Zucchini
Applesauce Cake

Borscht
Cheesy French Bread
Green Salad with Creamy
  Herb Dressing

Split Pea Soup
Cornbread
French Vegetable Salad

Tortilla Casserole
Mexican Salad Bowl
Brown Rice

Cuban Black Bean Soup
Mexican Salad Bowl
Spanish Rice

Wonderful Crock Pot
  Lentils
Bulgur Wheat
Spinach Salad with Creamy
  Herb Dressing

Spinach Pie
French Vegetable Salad

Tomato Soup
Tofu Cornbread
Salad with Green Goddess
  Dressing

Eggplant Parmesan
Brown Rice
Spinach Salad

Skillet Green Bean Pie
Cornbread
Salad with Basic Vinaigrette
  Dressing

Cheesy Scalloped Potatoes
Borscht
Green Salad with Green
  Goddess Dressing

Lasagna
Hot Herb Bread
Salad with Basic Vinaigrette
  Dressing

Seasonal eating refers to using fresh vegetables and fruits during the season when they are naturally available. The advantages of seasonal eating are many:

1. Seasonal foods cost less. Foods that are available out of their normal season must be stored in expensive warehouse space under refrigeration, or shipped great distances from climates much different from ours. Storage and shipping costs are passed along to you, the consumer.

2. Seasonal foods are more nutritious. Important vitamins are lost while fruits and vegetables sit in storage. Furthermore, some vitamins and minerals are lost when foods undergo any type of processing—including canning, freezing, or dehydrating.

3. Seasonal foods taste better. If you've ever eaten a tomato in January, you already know this.

4. Seasonal foods take less energy to produce. Storage, refrigeration, shipping, and processing all require significant amounts of energy, which are not required by seasonal foods.

HINTS FOR EATING SEASONALLY

1. Look for the produce that is most abundant and lowest in price; this is generally the food that is in season.
2. Use canned, frozen, and dried fruits and vegetables as little as possible. If a fresh alternative is available, use it.
3. Grow your own fruits and vegetables. This way you can be assured of fresh, seasonal produce.
4. Use the chart on page 29 to determine which foods are in season at different times of the year.

VEGETABLES BY THE SEASON

Cool-season vegetables make their best growth before, or after, summer temperatures peak. Where summers are cool, some of the cool-season vegetables may be grown year round.

Warm-season vegetables, also known as summer vegetables, grow best in climates with warm to hot days and fairly warm nights (night temperatures over 60 degrees).

Cool-Season Vegetables

Artichoke
Asparagus
Broad bean
Beet
Broccoli
Brussels sprouts
Cabbage
Carrot
Cauliflower
Celery
Chinese cabbage
Chive
Endive

Garlic
Kohlrabi
Leek
Lettuce
Onion
Parsnip
Pea
Potato
Radish
Rhubarb
Shallots
Spinach
Turnip

Warm-Season Vegetables

Beans
Corn
Cucumber
Eggplant
Melons
Okra

Peppers
Squash
Sweet potato
Swiss chard
Tomato
All berries

Sprouting is an easy way to begin growing some of your own food, and an inexpensive way of having fresh vegetables on a year-round basis.

The remarkable thing about sprouts is that they are higher in certain nutrients than the seeds from which they come. Some of these nutrients include: B vitamins (especially thiamin and riboflavin), vitamin C, vitamin A, vitamin E, vitamin K, and lysine and tryptophan—two essential amino acids.

Most beans, nuts, and seeds can be sprouted using the method described below; however, some are easier to grow than others. The chart on page 31 lists these.

Method:

1. Select the seeds—it is best to purchase seeds from a food store rather than from a nursery, as nursery seeds are often treated with mercury and fungicides.

2. Place the amount of seed indicated on the chart (page 31) in a wide-mouth quart jar. Cover the jar with a piece of mesh fabric (cheesecloth, nylon mesh, or an old nylon stocking will do). Secure the fabric with a mason ring or a rubber band.

3. Rinse the seeds two or three times with lukewarm water, then fill the jar half full of water and soak the seeds overnight.

4. Drain the seeds (give the water to your plants or use it in soup—it's full of nutrients), and rinse two to three times with lukewarm water. Tilt the jar to remove all excess water, then shake the jar to distribute the seeds evenly, and lay it on its side in a fairly dark place.

5. Rinse the seeds twice a day (morning and night when you do the dishes), until the sprouts are

desired size. To make alfalfa sprouts green place them in indirect sunlight for a day.

6. Store mature sprouts in the refrigerator. They will keep best if you rinse and drain them thoroughly once a day.

SPROUT GROWING

Type of Sprout	Amount of Seed	Yield (cups)	Rinses per Day	Edible Length (inches)	Days Until Ready
Aduki beans	1 cup	2	2	1	3–4
Alfalfa	1 Tbsp.	4	2–3	2	3–5
Chia	1 Tbsp.	2	2	⅛–1½	2–4
Cress	1 Tbsp.	1½	2	1½	3–4
Lentils	1 cup	4	2–3	1	3–4
Wheat	1 cup	4	2	½	2–3
Rye	1 cup	4	2	½	2–3
Radish	1 Tbsp.	1½	2	½	2–3
Mung*	1 cup	4	2–3	2	4–5

*Mung bean sprouts are the typical bean sprout used in Chinese cooking. They are a bit tricky to grow, as they must be kept in the dark and rinsed and drained thoroughly. They are included here because they are so common.

PROTEIN CONTENT OF RECIPES

The following chart shows the approximate amount of protein in an average portion for each of the recipes in this book. It should be noted that protein complementarity is not taken into account in these figures, so the actual protein of each recipe will be slightly higher than shown.

	Quantity	Protein (grams)
BREAKFASTS		
Whole-Wheat Pancakes	1 3-in. pancake	5
Cornmeal Flapjacks	1 3-in. pancake	4
French Pancake	½ recipe	14
Multigrain Waffles	1 waffle	12
Granola	½ cup	7
Familia	½ cup	7
Scrambled Tofu	½ cup	8
Stewed Prunes	¼ cup	2
Prune Whip	¼ cup	4
Yogurt Shake	1½ cups (approx.)	11
SOUPS		
Borscht	1½ cups	2
Cream of Spinach Soup	1 cup	9
Cuban Black Bean Soup	1 cup	15
Golden Mushroom Soup	1 cup	5
Tomato Vegetable Soup	1 cup	4
Green Vegetable Soup	1½ cups	5
Lentil Soup	1 cup	15
Spicy Carrot Soup	1 cup	6
Split Pea Soup	1 cup	12
Tomato Soup	1 cup	5

SALADS, SPREADS, AND SAUCES

Avocado-Stuffed Zucchini . . . . . . ½ zucchini 2
French Vegetable Salad . . . . 1 cup 2
Spinach Salad I (with eggs) . . . . . 1 serving 4
Spinach Salad II . . . . 1 serving 3
Guacamole . . . . ¼ cup 2
Cucumber Salad . . . . ¾ cup 2
Mexican Salad Bowl . . . . 1 serving 5
Greek Salad . . . . 1 serving 2
Brown Rice Salad (with eggs) . . . 1½ cups 8
Banana and Coconut Raita . . . . . ½ cup 2
Cucumber Raita . . . . ½ cup 4
Tabouli . . . . 1 cup 8
Tofu Salad Sandwich Spread . . . ⅓ cup 6
Hummus bi Tahini . . . . ½ cup 12
Soy Paté . . . . ½ cup 10
Peanut Butter and Apple
    Sandwich Spread . . . . ⅓ 12

BREADS

Whole-Wheat Bread . . . . 1 slice 2
Whole-Wheat Sandwich Buns . . 1 bun 9
Basic Biscuits . . . . 1 biscuit 4
Custard Cornbread . . . . 1 3 x 3-in. square 6
Tofu Cornbread . . . . 1 3 x 3-in. square 6
Cheesy French Bread . . . . 1 slice 6
Hot Herb Bread . . . . 1 slice 3
Bran Muffins . . . . 1 muffin 4
Boston Brown Bread . . . . 1 slice 4
Banana Bread . . . . 1 slice 3
Cranberry Nut Bread . . . . 1 slice 2
Corn Tortillas . . . . 1 medium tortilla 2
Chapatis . . . . 1 large chapati 3
Croutons . . . . ⅓ cup 2

ENTREES

Vegetable Quiche	1 slice	12
Spinach Pie	1 slice	13
Neat Loaf	1 slice	14
Vegieburgers	1 patty	8
Beanburgers	1 patty	7
Tofu Burgers	1 patty	8
Basic Cheese Soufflé	⅙ soufflé	16
Cheesy Scalloped Potatoes	1 serving	15
Skillet Green Bean Pie	1 serving	20
Zucchini Casserole	1 serving	26
Stuffed Eggplant	½ eggplant	8
Brown Rice Pizza	1 slice	7
Ratatouille	1½ cups	17
Corn Pone	1 serving	16
Peanut Spaghetti	1 serving	21
Wonderful Crock Pot Lentils	1 serving	19
Crock Pot Soybean Stew	1 serving	14
Zucchini Pizzas	1 pocket	6
Stuffed Chard or Cabbage Leaves	1 leaf	4
Deep-Dish Pizza	1 4 x 4-in. piece	21
Lasagna	1 3 x 3-in. square	22
Vegetable Sauce and Polenta	1 serving	7
Eggplant Parmesan	1 3 x 3-in. square	14
Eggplant Cannelloni	2 cannelloni	28
Mexican Rice Bread	1 serving	10
Chili Beans	1 cup	20
Refried Beans I	1 cup	8
Refried Beans II (without cheese)	1 cup	8
Eggplant Enchiladas	1 enchilada	9
Spanish Rice (without cheese)	¾ cup	4
Cheese Enchiladas	1 serving	14
Tortilla Casserole	1 3 x 3-in. square	12
Tofu-Stuffed Shells	2 shells	8
Fried Tofu	½ cup	7
Tofu Lasagna	1 3 x 3-in. square	11

34

Moussaka	1 3 x 3-in. square	18
Feijoada	1 cup	13
Mjeddrah	1 cup	10
Falafel	1 falafel	6
Vegetable Curry	1½ cups	8
Dal	¾ cup	12
Curried Rice	1 cup	4
Vegetable Spaghetti	2 cups	16
Chinese Fried Rice (with egg)	1 cup	6
Vegetables and Tofu	1 cup	16
Tofu Brown Rice Casserole	1 3 x 3-in. square	17
Broccoli Tofu Pie	1 slice	12
Vegetable Shishkabobs	¼ recipe	12

DESSERTS

Peanut Raisin/Carob Cookies	1 cookie	4
Whole-Wheat Tea Cookies	1 cookie	1
Orange Cream Cheese	1 Tbsp.	1
Granola Cookies	1 cookie	2
Applesauce Cake	1 2 x 2-in. square	4
Molasses Crumb Cake	1 2 x 2-in. wedge	4
Fruit Pemmican	total recipe	73
Banana Bonbons	1 bonbon	1
Flan	½ cup	6
Okara and Coconut Macaroons	1 cookie	1
Okara Tofu Spice Bars	1 2 x 2½-in. square	4
Yogurt Cheesecake	1 slice	8
Tofu Cheesecake	1 slice	9
Vanilla Ice Cream	1 cup	5
Frozen Yogurt	1 cup	3
Simple Honey Frosting	⅙ cup	4
Middle Eastern Date and Banana Dessert	1 2-in. wedge	8

Breakfasts

Most of us have been lectured to, at one time or another, about the importance of a good breakfast. Yet the average American breakfast remains a rather sorry affair. If we eat breakfast at all, we pick foods that are high in sugar, other refined carbohydrates, and fats. Highly sweetened cold cereals, jams and jellies, sweet rolls and doughnuts, syrups and honey, all contribute to making the all-American breakfast as loaded with sugar as any dessert.

Ideally, breakfast should provide plenty of unrefined carbohydrates as well as some protein. This type of meal supplies a steady source of energy for the morning's activities, as well as the raw materials necessary for body growth and maintenance. In addition, the fiber contained in unrefined carbohydrates is filling, and helps prevent the midmorning munchies.

On weekday mornings, when time is usually limited, whole-grain cereals, both hot and cold, make excellent breakfasts. If your family objects to hot cereal, try fixing it with a chopped apple, raisins, sunflower seeds or cashews, and cinnamon. Serve with a dab of butter and milk. Try different kinds of cereals—oats, polenta, bulgur wheat, brown rice—and different toppings: fresh fruit, yogurt, applesauce, or a combination of these. For cold cereals, try the granola or familia in this section, or use your own favorite recipe. If you use commercial granola, be aware that many popular brands are approximately half sugar. Whole-grain toast also makes an excellent breakfast. Try topping it with applesauce or other fruit purees, and serving it with a yogurt shake.

On weekends, when time is more available, you might try whole-grain pancakes or waffles, served with fresh fruit and yogurt. For a really hearty breakfast, biscuits and gravy, served with fried tofu and hot applesauce, is a real favorite.

WHOLE-WHEAT PANCAKES

The regular version of this recipe is made with three eggs and is delicious. If, however, you are trying to limit your consumption of eggs, you'll be pleased to know that the recipe can be made with two, one, or no eggs at all. Add one additional teaspoon of oil or butter for each egg omitted, and enough extra milk to make the batter the correct consistency.

1 cup whole-wheat flour
1 Tbsp. soy flour
½ tsp. baking powder
¼ tsp. salt
¼ tsp. cinnamon
1 Tbsp. poppy seeds (optional)

3 eggs, separated
1–1½ cups milk
1 Tbsp. oil or melted butter
1–2 Tbsp. honey
1 Tbsp. grated orange rind
½ cup chopped walnuts, or
    sunflower seeds (optional)

Combine the dry ingredients in one bowl. In another bowl, combine the egg yolks, milk, oil or butter, honey, orange rind, and walnuts.

Mix the wet and dry ingredients together. Beat the egg whites until stiff, and fold in gently.

Melt enough butter in a skillet to just cover the bottom of the pan. Pour batter into pan to make small cakes and cook first side until top is dry. Turn and cook second side briefly. Serve hot with fresh fruit and yogurt, applesauce and yogurt, or your own favorite topping.

Serves 4.

CORNMEAL FLAPJACKS

1 cup cornmeal
¾ cup whole-wheat pastry flour
½ tsp. salt
½ tsp. soda

¼ cup butter
2 Tbsp. honey
3 eggs, lightly beaten
1½–2 cups buttermilk or milk

Combine the dry ingredients in one bowl. In another, cream the butter and the honey together. Beat in the eggs and 1½ cups of the buttermilk or milk.

Add the wet to the dry ingredients, and stir just to blend. Add the rest of the milk if the batter is too thick.

Make small cakes on a greased griddle, and cook until tops of cakes are dry. Turn carefully and cook until bottoms are browned.

Serve hot, topped with applesauce or other favorite topping.

Makes about 2 dozen small cakes.

FRENCH PANCAKE

This is a glorious-looking creation as it comes out of the oven. However, it fades fast, so serve as quickly as possible. It is very easy to make, but you must use whole-wheat *pastry* flour or unbleached flour, or it won't rise.

> 3 Tbsp. butter
> ½ cup whole-wheat pastry
>   flour or unbleached flour
> ½ cup milk
> 2 eggs, lightly beaten
>
> pinch nutmeg
> ½ fresh lemon
> honey

Preheat oven to 425°.

Melt the butter in a 10-inch cast iron skillet.

Mix the flour, milk, and eggs, and pour into the buttered skillet. Sprinkle lightly with nutmeg.

Bake 15 minutes, until puffy and lightly browned on the edges.

To serve, squeeze the juice from the ½ lemon over the top, and drizzle with honey. Serve immediately with fresh fruit.

Serves 2 to 4.

MULTIGRAIN WAFFLES

1¼ cups whole-wheat pastry flour
¼ cup rolled oats
¼ cup bran
½ cup cornmeal
2 tsp. baking powder
¼ tsp. salt
½ cup chopped walnuts (optional)

2 eggs, separated
2 Tbsp. honey or brown sugar
¼ cup melted butter
1½ cups milk

Stir together the dry ingredients.

Separate the eggs, and beat the whites until they form stiff peaks. Set aside.

Beat the yolks together with the honey, melted butter, and milk, then stir this mixture into the dry ingredients.

Gently fold egg whites into the batter.

Spoon into a preheated waffle iron and cook until lightly browned.

Serve with fresh fruit and yogurt, or with Simple Honey Syrup (page 45).

Makes 6 medium waffles.

Variation: For pancakes, follow above recipe using only 1 tsp. baking powder and 2 tsp. melted butter.

GRANOLA

5 cups rolled oats
1 cup sesame seeds
1 cup wheat germ
1 cup whole-wheat flour
1 cup soy flour or powder
1 cup sunflower seeds
1 cup coconut
1 cup chopped almonds
¾ cup oil (I prefer safflower)
¾ cup honey
1 cup raisins
1 cup dates, pitted and chopped

Mix dry ingredients together.

Combine oil and honey in a saucepan over low heat until honey melts.

When honey is melted, add liquid to dry ingredients and mix thoroughly. Spread in a thin layer on flat baking sheet with edges, and bake at 300° until golden brown (20 to 25 minutes).

After the first 10 minutes, you should check and stir the granola every 10 minutes to keep it from burning around the edges.

Spread out to cool, and when cool, add the raisins and dates.

Store in an airtight container.

Makes 1 gallon.

FAMILIA

Traditionally, this whole-grain cereal is eaten uncooked, with milk or yogurt and lots of fruit added. You can also cook it, which only takes a few minutes, or try it my favorite way: with hot milk poured over it.

3 cups rolled oats
1 cup rolled wheat
¾ cup almonds, chopped
½ cup dried apple, chopped
1 cup wheat germ
½ cup raisins

Grind the oats and wheat in a food processor or blender until they are fairly fine; this may have to be done in two to three batches.

Chop and add the almonds and the dried apples.

Add the wheat germ and raisins, and mix well.

Store in an airtight container.

Makes about 6 cups.

HOT CEREAL IN A THERMOS

This is one of the easiest ways to prepare hot cereal—no burning, sticking, or boiling over, and the cereal is ready when you get up in the morning. Try using any of the following grains, singly or in combination:

> *rolled oats (old fashioned)*
> *rolled rye*
> *rolled wheat*
> *brown rice*
> *polenta*
> *barley*
> *cracked wheat*
> *millet*
> *buckwheat*

Preheat a 1-pint thermos by filling it with boiling water.

When the thermos is hot, pour out the water. Measure ¾ cup of cereal and put it in the thermos. Add salt if desired.

Fill the thermos with boiling water. Put the lid on it, shake it a few times, and lay it on its side. The cereal will be cooked in the morning.

Try adding some chopped apple, raisins, and cinnamon to the cereal, before adding the water, for a special treat.

If you have any problem with the cereal not being fully cooked in the morning, try wrapping the thermos in a bath towel.

Makes 2 or 3 servings.

SIMPLE HONEY SYRUP

⅔ cup honey
½ cup butter

Heat in a small saucepan until just melted.
  Serve over pancakes or waffles.

SCRAMBLED TOFU

This can be served like scrambled eggs, or as a taco filling,
in warmed corn tortillas with lettuce and other garnishes,
topped with taco sauce.

1 Tbsp. oil
¼ cup chopped onion
1 cup (8 oz.) tofu, crumbled
¼–½ tsp. turmeric (enough to
  make mixture pale yellow)
¼ tsp. cumin
pinch red pepper or cayenne
1 Tbsp. tamari soy

Sauté the onion in oil until it is golden, then add the
remaining ingredients and cook over medium heat until the
tofu is dry and just starts to brown, about 5 minutes.

  Variation: Sauté any of the following vegetables with the
onion, then proceed as above:

¼ cup diced bell pepper
1 stalk celery, sliced
1 small carrot, thinly sliced
1 small zucchini, thinly sliced

Serves 2 to 4.

STEWED PRUNES

Prunes are a delicious source of vitamin A, vitamin B-6, iron, and potassium, as well as much-needed fiber. Try stewed prunes for breakfast, or prune whip, which looks like chocolate pudding, for dinner.

>   1 cup dried prunes
>   1 cup water

Simmer prunes for 20 minutes, until tender. Serve hot or cold, plain, or with milk or cream.
   Serves 4.

PRUNE WHIP

This delicious pudding can be eaten with breakfast, or for dessert. Moderation is recommended!

>   1 cup stewed prunes
>   1/3 cup milk
>   2 Tbsp. prune juice (from stewing)
>   2 Tbsp. carob powder

Remove pits from prunes, then combine all ingredients in blender and blend until smooth.
   Makes 1½ to 2 cups.

SAUTÉED APPLES

These are delicious, along with yogurt, on top of pancakes.

>   *6 firm, tart apples (I like to use Pippins)*
>   *2 Tbsp. butter*
>   *sprinkling of cinnamon*

Without peeling them, core and slice the apples fairly thin.
   Melt the butter in a skillet, then add the apples and
sprinkle them with cinnamon. Cover and sauté over
medium-low heat until the apples are just tender (about 5
minutes).
   Serve immediately.
Serves 4 to 6.

YOGURT SHAKE

Try this for breakfast with a couple of slices of whole-
wheat toast; it is quite filling and provides complete
protein.

>   *1 ripe banana*
>   *2 Tbsp. wheat germ*
>   *1 Tbsp. orange juice concentrate*
>   *or ½ fresh orange, peeled*
>   *1 cup yogurt*
>   *crushed ice*

Place all ingredients in blender and blend until smooth.
Frozen bananas may be used in place of the ice. Try
adding other fruit as it is in season: berries, peaches,
pineapple, apricots, etc.
   Serves 1.

Soups

BORSCHT

2 large beets
2 medium potatoes
1 cup diced carrot
1 cup diced celery
1 cup diced onion
1 quart stock or water
2 cups chopped tomatoes
1 cup shredded cabbage
Sour cream or yogurt

Dice first five vegetables. Place in a kettle and add just enough water to cover. Simmer gently for 20 minutes.

Add stock, tomatoes, and cabbage. Simmer for 15 minutes.

Ladle into bowls, and top each bowl with a spoonful of sour cream or yogurt.

Serves 8 to 10.

CREAM OF SPINACH SOUP

1 lb. fresh spinach or 1 pkg. frozen
2 Tbsp. butter
$\frac{1}{4}$ cup finely chopped onion
4 Tbsp. whole-wheat flour
4 cups milk
$\frac{1}{2}$ tsp. salt
$\frac{1}{4}$ tsp. paprika
pinch nutmeg

If using fresh spinach: pick over and wash the spinach well. Steam until tender, then chop and drain.

If using frozen spinach, thaw and drain spinach.

Melt the butter and sauté the onion until it is golden. Add the flour and cook the mixture for 2 to 3 minutes, stirring constantly. Gradually whisk in the milk, then add the salt and seasonings.

Add the spinach and heat the soup thoroughly. Serve hot, topped with grated Parmesan cheese.

Serves 6.

CUBAN BLACK BEAN SOUP

1 lb. (2½ cups) black beans
6–8 cups water

5 cloves garlic, crushed
2 Tbsp. white vinegar
1½ tsp. cumin
1½ tsp. oregano
1 tsp. salt (or more to taste)

3 Tbsp. olive oil
1 large onion, chopped
1 large green bell pepper, chopped

RICE MARINADE:
1 cup cooked rice
2 Tbsp. finely chopped onion
2 Tbsp. white vinegar
1 Tbsp. olive oil

For soup: Soak beans overnight, if possible, then simmer, covered, until soft, about 1½ hours.

In a small bowl combine garlic, vinegar, cumin, oregano, and salt.

Sauté the onion and bell pepper in the oil until the onion is golden, then stir in garlic mixture and sauté 1 to 2 minutes more. Add to beans, cover, and simmer about 1 hour, stirring occasionally.

For marinade: Combine rice, onion, vinegar, and oil in a small bowl. Cover and marinate at least 2 hours at room temperature. Add a generous tablespoon of the rice mixture to each soup bowl just before serving.

Serves 6 to 8.

GOLDEN MUSHROOM SOUP

This is a wonderful soup—full of mushrooms.

> 2 Tbsp. butter or olive oil
> 2 cups chopped onion
> 1 lb. mushrooms, sliced
> 1½ tsp. dill weed
> 1 Tbsp. paprika
> pinch red pepper
> 2 Tbsp. tamari soy
> 2 cups water or stock
> 2 Tbsp. butter
> 3 Tbsp. whole-wheat flour
> 1 cup milk
>
> 2 tsp. lemon juice
> 4 Tbsp. red wine
> 2–4 Tbsp. sour cream

Melt the butter and sauté the onion in it or the oil until golden. Add the mushrooms, dill weed, paprika and red pepper, and sauté for 5 minutes, stirring frequently. Add the tamari and 1 cup of the stock, then cover and simmer for 15 minutes.

Melt 2 Tbsp. butter in a fairly large pan, and add the flour. Cook 2 to 3 minutes, then add the milk, stirring constantly. Simmer over low heat, stirring frequently, until the mixture is thick.

Stir in the mushrooms and remaining stock. Cover and simmer 15 minutes.

Just before serving, whisk in the lemon juice, red wine, and sour cream.

Serves 6.

TOMATO VEGETABLE SOUP

1 cup navy beans or small
 white beans
5 cups water or stock

2 Tbsp. olive oil
1 onion, chopped
4 cloves garlic, minced

1 carrot, sliced into rounds
1 stalk celery, sliced
1 bell pepper, diced
1 cup corn
½ cup parsley, finely chopped
1 28-oz. can tomatoes,
 chopped, with liquid
1 cup tomato sauce
½ tsp. basil
pinch cayenne

1 Tbsp. tamari soy
¼ cup red wine (optional)

Cook the beans in the water until they are tender, about 2 hours.

In a large kettle, sauté the onion and garlic in the oil until the onion is just turning golden. Add all the remaining ingredients except the tamari soy and the red wine and simmer at least 1 hour, or until the carrots are tender.

Just before serving, pour in the tamari and wine.

Serves 6 to 8.

GREEN VEGETABLE SOUP

2 Tbsp. butter
½ onion, chopped
2 stalks celery, diced

6 cups water or stock
¾ cup green split peas
1 bay leaf

6 cups shredded zucchini
¼ tsp. basil
pinch red pepper
2 tsp. salt

½ lb. spinach
1 Tbsp. fresh parsley

Melt the butter in a kettle, and sauté the onion and celery until the onion is golden.

Add 4 cups of the water/stock, the split peas, and the bay leaf. Bring to a boil, then cover and simmer over low heat for about 45 minutes.

Grate the zucchini, and add it, along with the remaining stock and seasonings. Simmer for 10 minutes.

Remove the bay leaf, and puree the soup in a blender. Return it to the soup pot.

Wash the spinach, and chop it very fine. Add it, along with the parsley, to the soup, and cook over medium heat for about 10 more minutes.

Serve with a sprinkling of paprika on top.

Serves 10.

LENTIL SOUP

3 cups lentils
7 cups water
1 tsp. salt

1 cup chopped onion
2 cloves garlic, minced
2 Tbsp. olive oil
1 cup chopped celery
1 cup chopped carrot

2 Tbsp. dry red wine
2 Tbsp. lemon juice
1½ Tbsp. molasses
1 Tbsp. wine vinegar

Put the lentils in a pot with the water and the salt, and bring to a boil. Reduce heat, cover, and simmer for 3 hours.

Saute the onion and garlic in the oil until the onion is golden, then add the celery and carrot and cook 2-3 minutes more. Add to the cooked lentils, and simmer 1 hour.

About 30 minutes before serving, add the red wine, lemon juice, molasses, and vinegar.

Serves 6 to 8.

SPICY CARROT SOUP

This is a delicious and different soup: sweet, spicy, and creamy all at the same time.

1 onion, chopped
2 Tbsp. olive oil
1 lb. carrots, chopped
  (about 4 cups)
2 cloves garlic, minced
½ tsp. mustard seeds
½ tsp. turmeric
½ tsp. ginger
½ tsp. cumin
¼ tsp. cinnamon

⅛ tsp. cayenne
½ tsp. salt
1 Tbsp. lemon juice
1 cup water

3 Tbsp. butter
3 Tbsp. flour
4 cups milk
1 Tbsp. honey

yogurt

Sauté the onion in the olive oil until golden. Add the carrots, garlic, spices, salt, and lemon juice. Cook 2 to 3 minutes, stirring constantly.

Add the water, cover tightly, and simmer until the carrots are tender, about 20 minutes.

Puree the mixture in a blender or sieve, adding a small amount of the milk if necessary. Be careful to fill the blender no more than half full; start it on a low speed, and hold the top on tightly. Otherwise, the hot mixture can "explode" and splatter you and everything in sight!

In a saucepan, melt the butter, and add the flour. Cook for 2 to 3 minutes, stirring often. Add the milk, stirring constantly with a whisk. Cook the sauce over medium heat, stirring fairly constantly, until it is very hot.

Combine the sauce with the carrot puree, and heat until very hot, about 10 minutes.

Serve hot with a spoonful of yogurt on top.

Serves 8.

SPLIT PEA SOUP

2 cups split peas
10 cups water

2 Tbsp. oil
1 cup finely chopped carrots
1 cup finely chopped celery
1 cup finely chopped onion
2 cloves garlic, minced
½ tsp. marjoram
½ tsp. basil
¼ tsp. cumin
pinch cayenne
½–1 tsp. salt or 1 Tbsp. light miso*
black pepper to taste (optional)
2 Tbsp. butter

Put the split peas in a pot with the water, bring them to a boil, then lower heat and simmer for 1 hour. Skim off any foam which develops.

Sauté the vegetables in the oil for about 5 minutes, then add the herbs and spices (except the salt, pepper, and butter), and sauté another five minutes.

Add the vegetable mixture to the split peas, along with the salt (or miso), and simmer, stirring occasionally, for about 45 minutes.

Add the pepper and butter, and serve very hot.
Serves 6 to 8.

*Miso is a fermented soybean paste, which adds saltiness and flavor.

TOMATO SOUP

1 large onion, finely chopped
3 cloves garlic, minced
1 Tbsp. olive oil
1 Tbsp. butter
1 tsp. dill weed
⅛ tsp. basil
pinch red pepper
6 cups canned tomatoes,
  chopped, with liquid
1 Tbsp. honey
¼ cup sour cream

yogurt
parsley, chopped
green onions, chopped

Sauté the onion and garlic in the combined oil and butter until the onion turns golden. Add the dill, basil, pepper, tomatoes, and honey. Cover and simmer over low heat for 45 minutes.

Whisk in sour cream.

Serve hot, garnished with a spoonful of yogurt and a sprinkling of chopped parsley and green onion.

Serves 6.

Salads, Spreads, and Sauces

ANTIPASTO

Antipasto platters are traditional Italian appetizers, consisting of marinated and raw vegetables, and marinated beans. The antipasto can be a meal in itself, if served with bread and cheese (and perhaps a bit of wine). It can be arranged artfully on a single platter, or placed in several smaller dishes—the only limit is your imagination! Antipasto is colorful and fun to assemble, and it's easy because most of the dishes are served cold.

THE VEGETABLES: Choose any of the following (try to get a variety of colors) and prepare as directed.

Cauliflower and broccoli: Break into small flowerets, and steam until just tender. Add, while still hot, to marinade (see below).

Carrots: Cut into traditional carrot sticks, and steam until just tender. Add, still hot, to marinade.

Green beans: Snip ends off fresh green beans; steam whole beans until just tender, then add, still hot, to marinade.

Peppers: Cut green and red bell peppers into strips, and marinate.

Artichokes: Steam artichokes about 40 minutes (until tender). Split in half lengthwise, remove fuzz, and marinate, face down, in a shallow pan. Baste them as they marinate.

Asparagus: Steam until just tender, and marinate while still hot.

Cucumbers: Cut attractively and marinate or leave plain.

Red Onion: Thinly slice into rings and marinate.

Radishes: Cut attractively and marinate or leave plain.

Beets: Steam until just tender, and marinate while still hot.

Mushrooms: Clean and remove stems; steam caps 5 minutes, then marinate.

THE BEANS: Garbanzos or kidney beans are the best. For each cup of dry beans, use 3 cups of water. Simmer until the beans are just tender (for garbanzos, about 3 hours; for kidney beans, about 1½ hours). Drain the cooked beans *(save the water for soups, rice, etc.!)*, and marinate while still hot. Chill several hours.

THE MARINADE:

> ¾ cup oil (use all or part olive oil)
> ¾ cup cider or wine vinegar
> ½–1 tsp. salt
> 2 cloves garlic, minced
> pinch of basil
> pinch of tarragon
> freshly ground black pepper (optional)

Mix all ingredients in a blender, or with a whisk, until creamy. This is enough marinade for two pounds of vegetables.

AVOCADO-STUFFED ZUCCHINI

These delicious appetizers will take the place of a salad if you wish, and are perfect on a warm day.

> 6 medium-small zucchini
> 2 ripe avocados
> 1 Tbsp. fresh lemon juice
> 1 Tbsp. wine vinegar
> 1 Tbsp. fresh basil
> ½–1 tsp. salt
> paprika

Trim the stems off the zucchini and cut them in half lengthwise. Steam them for 5 minutes, until they are just barely tender, then plunge them into ice water for a minute. While zucchini is steaming, peel and mash the avocados.

Scoop out the zucchini pulp with a spoon, leaving a shell about ¼-in. thick. Allow the pulp to drain in a colander for 10 minutes.

Mash the drained pulp, along with the avocado, then mix in the lemon juice, vinegar, fresh basil, and salt.

Spread the avocado mixture in the zucchini shells and sprinkle with paprika. Chill for 1 to 2 hours before serving.

Serves 6.

FRENCH VEGETABLE SALAD

2 large new potatoes, washed
3 large carrots, washed
1 cup fresh green beans,
  washed and cut into 1-in. pieces
1 cup freshly shelled peas
½ head fresh cauliflower
1 large cucumber

1 cup Vinaigrette Sauce,
  approximately (see page 64)

salt and pepper to taste
chopped fresh parsley

Dice the potatoes and carrots into 1-in. cubes. Steam over boiling water, together with the green beans, until just tender (about 10 minutes).

Steam the peas until just tender, about 3 minutes.

Break the cauliflower into tiny flowerets and cook the same way, until it is just barely tender. Cool all the cooked vegetables.

Peel the cucumber (if it is waxed), or score and dice it. When the cooked vegetables are cool, add them to the cucumber, along with the Vinaigrette Sauce, and salt and pepper if desired. Toss to mix well.

Chill the salad for an hour or two, then toss again and serve on beds of lettuce with a garnish of freshly chopped parsley.

Serves 10.

VINAIGRETTE SAUCE

½ cup white wine vinegar
1 Tbsp. lemon juice
2 tsp. Dijon mustard
2 cloves garlic, minced
½ cup olive oil
salt and freshly ground black pepper

Mix together the vinegar, lemon juice, mustard, and garlic.

Add the olive oil, a little at a time, beating with a whisk until the mixture is homogeneous (creamy looking).

Add salt and pepper to taste.

This is enough dressing for one pound of vegetables.

(This dressing may also be made in a blender. Simply add all of the ingredients and blend at high speed about 20 seconds.)

SESAME SAUCE FOR COOKED VEGETABLES

2 Tbsp. sesame seeds
2 Tbsp. oil
2 Tbsp. vinegar
2 Tbsp. soy sauce
2 Tbsp. honey

Toast sesame seeds by placing in an ungreased cast iron skillet over medium heat until they begin to turn brown and pop. Stir once or twice.

Combine toasted sesame seeds with remaining ingredients in a small saucepan and bring to a boil over medium heat.

Pour over cooked vegetables and toss gently.

Serve immediately.

GUACAMOLE

2 large avocados
¼ cup lemon juice
¼ cup onion
2 medium tomatoes
4 Tbsp. chopped, mild green chiles
½ tsp. salt (or more to taste)

Peel avocados, and mash with a fork in a small bowl. Add the lemon juice immediately, as this prevents browning.

Chop the onions very fine, and the tomatoes fairly fine. Add these, along with the chiles and the salt. Mix thoroughly, and serve chilled (if you can wait), with tortilla chips, tostadas, burritos, or just about anything.

Makes 1¼ cups.

SPINACH SALAD I

1 lb. fresh spinach
¼ lb. fresh mushrooms (with
    caps still closed)
Croutons (see page 88)
Creamy Herb Dressing (see page 72)
2 hard-boiled eggs, finely
    chopped (optional)

Wash the spinach carefully, trim off the stems, and dry the leaves. Tear into bite-sized pieces.

Clean the mushrooms and slice. Add to spinach. Toss with Creamy Herb Dressing and top with croutons, and chopped egg if desired.

Serves 6.

SPINACH SALAD II

The Orange Sesame Dressing makes this salad unique.

> 2 yams
> ¼–½ head cabbage, shredded
> 1 large bunch spinach

Wash yams and steam until tender (about 20 minutes). Slice into half moons and chill.

Steam shredded cabbage briefly, so it is still crunchy, and chill.

Wash and dry spinach leaves, remove stems, and tear into bite-sized pieces.

When the vegetables are cool, mix them together, add Orange Sesame Dressing, and toss well.

ORANGE SESAME DRESSING

> ¼ cup sesame seeds
> ¼ cup olive oil
> 2 Tbsp. lemon juice
> 1 Tbsp. vinegar
> ¼ tsp. salt
> ⅛ tsp. celery seed
> ⅛ tsp. cumin
> ⅛ tsp. paprika
> juice of 1 orange

Toast the sesame seeds by heating in a dry skillet over medium heat. Grind them in a blender, then add the remaining ingredients and blend.

Serves 8.

CUCUMBER SALAD

A lovely, cool salad for warm days and spicy meals.

> 2 large cucumbers, peeled (if
>   waxed) and thinly sliced
> 1 slice onion
> ½ tsp. dill
> ¼ cup vinegar
> water
>
> 1 cup yogurt
> ⅛ tsp. turmeric
> ½ tsp. salt

Put the cucumber slices, onion, dill, and vinegar in a bowl. Add enough water to just cover cucumbers (up to 1 cup), stir, and allow to marinate at least 30 minutes.

At the end of this time, drain, and discard onion.

Mix the yogurt, turmeric, and salt, and pour over marinated cucumber slices. Toss and serve on beds of fresh lettuce.

Serves 6.

MEXICAN SALAD BOWL

¾ cup cooked kidney beans
1 bunch leafy lettuce
1 avocado, cubed
1 green pepper, diced
1 tomato, diced
3 green onions, finely chopped
½ cup grated Cheddar cheese

DRESSING:
¼ cup olive oil
2 Tbsp. lemon juice
2 Tbsp. vinegar
¼ tsp. salt
¼ tsp. mustard powder
¼ tsp. paprika
¼ tsp. oregano
⅛ tsp. cumin
1 Tbsp. catsup

Mix all dressing ingredients together in a jar or bowl.

Chill and marinate the kidney beans in ¼ cup dressing. Wash and dry the lettuce, tear into bite-sized pieces, and place in a bowl.

Toss the remaining vegetables with the remaining dressing. Just before eating, add the vegetables and the beans to the lettuce, and toss lightly.

Sprinkle cheese over top and serve.

Serves 8.

GREEK SALAD

What makes this salad "Greek" is the use of lemon juice and oregano in the dressing—a traditional Greek flavor combination.

1 lb. lettuce (romaine, red, butter)
1 large cucumber, sliced
1 large tomato, cut in wedges
1 bell pepper, seeded and sliced
½ small red onion, thinly sliced
½–1 cup sliced radishes
½ cup sliced black olives
    (Greek, if available)

DRESSING:
¼ cup olive oil
3 Tbsp. lemon juice
½ tsp. dried oregano
¼ tsp. salt
1 clove garlic, minced
pinch black pepper (optional)

2 oz. (about ¼ cup) Feta
    cheese, crumbled

Place vegetables together in a large bowl.

Combine dressing ingredients in a small bowl, and beat with a fork or whisk until well blended. Pour over salad and toss.

Top with crumbled Feta cheese.

Serves 8.

BROWN RICE SALAD

8 cups cooked brown rice
  (preferably long-grain)
1 red onion, minced
1 large bell pepper, diced
1 cup thinly sliced celery
1 large carrot, coarsely grated
1 cup finely shredded cabbage
1 large tomato, diced
⅓ cup finely chopped parsley
2 cups green peas, lightly steamed
1 Tbsp. curry powder
¼ cup mayonnaise

DRESSING:
¼ cup olive oil
¼ cup vinegar (white wine is nice)
1 Tbsp. Dijon mustard
½ tsp. salt
3 cloves garlic, minced

2 cucumbers, sliced
4 hard-cooked eggs, sliced (optional)

Combine the rice with all the vegetables except the cucumbers. Mix in the curry powder and the mayonnaise.

Blend the ingredients for the dressing, pour over salad, and toss well.

Chill for several hours, or overnight, then mound on a serving platter and surround with the cucumbers and sliced eggs.

Makes 12 generous servings.

BANANA AND COCONUT RAITA

Raitas are served with curries, to cool everything down. These are two of my favorites.

2 Tbsp. butter
1 tsp. mustard seeds
1/8–1/4 tsp. cayenne
1/2 cup unsweetened coconut
2 ripe bananas, mashed
1/4–1/2 tsp. salt
1/2 tsp. honey
2 cups yogurt

Melt the butter in a medium-sized saucepan, and add the mustard seeds. Stir the seeds over medium heat for a minute or two, then stir in the cayenne.

After another minute, add the coconut and bananas, remove from heat, and stir quickly.

Add the remaining ingredients, beat together slightly with a fork and chill for several hours before serving. Serves 8.

CUCUMBER RAITA

1 large cucumber
2–3 Tbsp. finely chopped onion
2 cups yogurt
1/4 tsp. ground cumin
salt
1/8 tsp. cayenne (optional)

Peel the cucumber and grate it coarsely. Stir it together with the onion and yogurt.

Heat the ground cumin in a small pan, then remove it from the heat and add it to the yogurt mixture. Add the cayenne and salt to taste, and mix thoroughly. Chill well before serving.

Serves 6 to 8.

TABOULI

1½ cups uncooked bulgur wheat
3¼ cups boiling water
⅓ cup dry garbanzo beans
   (chick peas), cooked and
   drained
¾ cup chopped green onions
¾ cup finely chopped parsley
⅓ cup chopped fresh mint leaves
3 medium tomatoes, chopped
½ cup lemon juice
¼ cup olive oil
½–1 tsp. salt
1 clove garlic, minced

lettuce leaves
parsley sprigs

Put the bulgur in a large bowl and pour the boiling water over it. Cover and let stand 2 to 3 hours, until wheat is light and fluffy. Drain off excess liquid.

Add all remaining ingredients, except lettuce and parsley. Stir to mix, then chill 2 to 3 hours.

Serve on lettuce leaves, garnished with sprigs of fresh parsley.

Serves 6.

BASIC VINAIGRETTE DRESSING

½ cup vinegar
2 tsp. Dijon mustard
2 cloves garlic, minced
½ cup olive oil
salt to taste
pepper (optional)

Mix together the vinegar, mustard, and garlic.

Add the olive oil, beating constantly with a whisk until the mixture is creamy.

Add salt to taste (about ½ tsp.), and pepper if desired.
Makes 1 cup.

CREAMY HERB DRESSING

½ cup red wine vinegar
½ cup olive oil
½ tsp. basil
½ tsp. oregano
½ tsp. salt
⅛ tsp. pepper (optional)
2 cloves garlic, minced
½ cup buttermilk or yogurt

Combine all ingredients, and beat with a whisk, or in a blender, until smooth.
Makes 1 cup.

GREEN GODDESS DRESSING

¼ cup mayonnaise
½ cup yogurt
2–3 Tbsp. chopped fresh parsley
1 tsp. chopped fresh chives
2 tsp. vinegar
¼ tsp. basil

Place all ingredients in blender and blend well.
Makes about ¾ cup.

TOFU SALAD SANDWICH SPREAD

1 cup tofu (1 cup = ½ lb.)
1 green onion
2 Tbsp. mayonnaise
1 Tbsp. finely chopped mild,
  green chiles
¼ cup sunflower seeds
2 tsp. pickle relish
1 tsp. tamari soy
¼ tsp. cumin
¼ tsp. turmeric
⅛ tsp. garlic powder

Mash the tofu into fairly small pieces. Chop the green
onion (use both white and green parts) quite fine, and add
it to the tofu.

Add the remaining ingredients and mix thoroughly.
Serve on whole-wheat bread with lettuce, sprouts, tomatoes, or any of your other favorite garnishes.

Makes enough for 4 sandwiches.

HUMMUS bi TAHINI

    3 cups cooked garbanzo beans
       (chick peas) or 1¼ cups dry
    4 large cloves garlic, minced or
       crushed
    5 Tbsp. lemon juice
    ½ tsp. salt
    2 Tbsp. finely chopped fresh parsley
    1 carrot, grated
    ½ tsp. cumin
    ½ tsp. paprika
    ½ cup tahini (sesame-seed butter)

If using dry garbanzo beans, cook in 3–4 cups water for about 3 hours.

Mash the cooked garbanzo beans until they are very smooth. Add the remaining ingredients and mix well. The hummus should have the consistency of mayonnaise.

Serve on bread with mayonnaise and assorted vegetables: sprouts, cucumbers, lettuce, tomatoes, etc.

Makes 6 to 8 sandwiches.

SOY PATÉ

    2¾ cups cooked soybeans
    2 Tbsp. oil (olive is good)
    2½ Tbsp. soy sauce
    ¼ tsp. thyme
    ¼ tsp. sage
    ¼ tsp. cumin
    4 Tbsp. chopped fresh parsley
    ¼–½ tsp. garlic powder
    1–2 tsp. pureed beet
       (optional—for color only)

Mash or blend soybeans until they are smooth, then add remaining ingredients. Adjust seasonings to taste.

Serve over rice or bulgur, with vegetable salads, or as a sandwich spread.

Makes 6 sandwiches.

PEANUT BUTTER AND APPLE
SANDWICH SPREAD

This spread is much less dry than regular peanut butter. It is also lower in fat, and naturally sweet.

> 1 large apple, finely chopped
>   or grated (I use Pippins)
> ½ cup peanut butter
> ¼ cup raisins

Chop apple in a food processor or grinder, or grate by hand. Mix thoroughly with peanut butter and raisins.
  Makes about 1 cup.

MUSHROOM GRAVY

A gravy for all occasions. Try this with Neat Loaf or Beanburgers. For a really hearty breakfast, serve it over Basic Biscuits and Fried Tofu.

> 4 Tbsp. butter
> ½ cup finely chopped onion
> 2 cups sliced mushrooms
> 1 clove garlic, crushed
>
> 4 Tbsp. whole-wheat flour
>
> 2 cups milk
> 2–3 Tbsp. soy sauce
> ½ tsp. paprika
> 1 Tbsp. sherry (optional)

Melt the butter and sauté the onion until it is golden. Add the sliced mushrooms and garlic and continue cooking until the onion is browned.
  Stir in the flour. Add the milk, stirring constantly, and the remaining ingredients, and continue cooking over medium heat until the gravy is thick. Additional milk may be added if the gravy becomes too thick.
  Serves 4.

Breads

WHOLE-WHEAT BREAD

2 Tbsp. dry yeast
½ cup warm water (about 105°)
5 cups hot tap water (about 120°)
12 cups whole-wheat flour
1 Tbsp. salt
½ cup oil or melted butter
½ cup honey

Sprinkle the yeast onto the ½ cup warm water, and let it stand 10 to 15 minutes. The yeast should get very bubbly and increase in volume. If it does not, it will not make the bread rise, as it is too old and tired. Start over with new yeast.

Combine the hot water and 7 cups of the flour. Add the salt, oil, and honey, and mix until the dough becomes fairly elastic.

Add the yeast and blend thoroughly.

Add 4-5 cups more flour (the amount varies depending on how fresh the flour is—fresher flour is moister), and knead on a floured board for 10 to 20 minutes, until the dough is very smooth and elastic. (When kneading, try to work with the dough as moist as possible. If it is too dry, the bread will not rise as well). Divide into 4 pieces.

Mold dough into loaves on an oiled cookie sheet and place in greased loaf pans. Place in a warm spot to rise until dough is double in volume, for about one hour.

Bake at 350° for 40 to 45 minutes. Bread is done when it sounds hollow when tapped. Remove from pans and place on rack to cool.

Makes 4 loaves.

WHOLE-WHEAT SANDWICH BUNS

2 Tbsp. dry yeast
¼ cup lukewarm water

1 cup boiling water
1 cup bulgur or cracked wheat

¼ cup honey
2 Tbsp. oil or melted butter
1½ tsp. salt
1½ cups small-curd cottage
   cheese (low-fat)
3 eggs, lightly beaten

5–6 cups whole-wheat flour

Dissolve the yeast in the lukewarm water and allow to stand 15 minutes. The mixture should become quite bubbly. If it does not, start with fresh yeast.

Pour the boiling water over the cracked wheat. Let stand 15 minutes, then add the honey, oil or butter, salt, cottage cheese, and beaten eggs.

When the yeast is bubbly, add it to the cracked-wheat mixture and blend.

Add 3 cups of the flour, and beat well, so that the dough is stretchy.

Add enough of the remaining flour to make a moderately stiff dough, and knead for 10 minutes.

Put dough into a greased bowl and turn once to grease top. Let it rise until double, about 1½ hours.

Punch dough down, knead briefly, and divide it into 20 equal pieces. Make each piece into a ball, flatten, and place on a greased cooky sheet. Cover and let rise until puffy and almost double, about 45 minutes.

Bake at 375° for 15 minutes. Cool on wire racks.
Makes 20 buns.

Note: You can also shape this into two loaves of bread, if desired. Bake at 375° for 45 to 50 minutes.

BASIC BISCUITS

2 cups flour (I use whole- wheat pastry flour)
2 tsp. baking powder
½ tsp. salt
¼ cup butter
½–¾ cup milk

Blend together flour, baking powder, and salt. Cut in butter until mixture resembles coarse cornmeal. Add enough milk to make a workable dough, then knead 15 times.

Roll dough out about ½-in. thick, and cut into rounds with a biscuit cutter or the open end of a glass.

Bake at 450° for 12 to 15 minutes.

Makes 12 biscuits.

CUSTARD CORNBREAD

This unusual cornbread has a custardy layer in the middle

1 cup coarse cornmeal or polenta
½ cup whole-wheat flour
½ cup whole-wheat pastry flour
2 tsp. baking powder
½ tsp. salt

1 egg, lightly beaten
¼ cup melted butter
¼–½ cup honey
3 cups milk or buttermilk

Mix dry ingredients in one bowl, and wet ingredients in another. Add the dry ingredients to the wet, and stir just to blend.

Pour into a greased and floured 9 x 9-in. baking dish, and bake at 350° for 50 minutes. Cut into squares and serve hot.

Serves 8.

TOFU CORNBREAD

This cornbread is a bit moister, and probably chewier, than what you're used to. It is also packed with protein.

½ lb. tofu
2 eggs
3 Tbsp. melted butter, or oil
¼ cup honey
1 cup milk

1½ cups cornmeal
¼ cup whole-wheat flour
1 tsp. salt
1½ tsp. baking powder
½ tsp. baking soda

Combine wet ingredients in a blender and blend until smooth.

Mix together the dry ingredients in a large bowl. Add the tofu mixture and stir until just blended. Pour into a greased and floured 9 x 9-in. baking dish, and bake at 425° for 25 to 30 minutes. Serve hot.

Serves 9.

CHEESY FRENCH BREAD

1¼ cups grated Cheddar cheese
½ cup chopped green onion
½-¾ cup mayonnaise

1 loaf French bread

Mix together shredded cheese and chopped onion; add enough mayonnaise to make a spreadable mixture (not wet).

Cut loaf of bread in half, lengthwise, then into thick slices, without cutting through the bottom crust. Spread with the cheese mixture, and bake at 350° for 20 minutes.

HOT HERB BREAD

½ cup butter
1 Tbsp. dried parsley
2 cloves garlic, minced
½ tsp. thyme
¼ tsp. oregano
¼ tsp. basil
¼ tsp. marjoram

1 loaf French bread

Let the butter stand at room temperature until soft. When it is soft, work in the garlic and herbs, until the mixture is smooth.

Slice the bread just to the bottom crust, but not through it. Butter one side of each slice with the herb butter.

Wrap the loaf in foil and heat it in a 325° oven for about 15 minutes.

BRAN MUFFINS

2 cups whole-wheat flour
1½ cups wheat bran
½ tsp. salt
1¼ tsp. baking soda
½ tsp. nutmeg
1 tsp. cinnamon
1 heaping Tbsp. grated orange rind
1 cup chopped apple
½ cup raisins
½ cup chopped nuts

juice of 1 orange (about ½ cup)
1½ cups buttermilk
1 egg, lightly beaten
½ cup molasses
2 Tbsp. oil

Mix together dry ingredients, then stir in fruits and nuts.

Combine the liquid ingredients, then stir those into the flour mixture with a few quick strokes.

Pour into greased muffin pans, filling them two-thirds full, and bake at 350° for 25 minutes.

Makes about 24 muffins.

BOSTON BROWN BREAD

This bread is moist and tender, and wonderfully easy to mix. It can take up to three hours to cook, however, as it is steamed, so start early.

> 1½ cups whole-wheat flour
> ½ cup rye flour
> 1 cup cornmeal
> 1½ tsp. baking powder
> ½ tsp. baking soda
> ¾ tsp. salt
>
> 2 cups buttermilk or 2 cups milk
> + 4 Tbsp. vinegar
> ¼ cup low-fat or skim milk
> ½ cup molasses
> ½ cup raisins

Grease and dust with cornmeal or flour a 2-lb. coffee can, or three 20-oz. cans, and set aside.

Mix dry ingredients in a large bowl. In a separate bowl mix liquid ingredients. Add liquid to the dry ingredients, and stir just enough to moisten thoroughly.

Fill cans ⅔ full, and cover with foil, secured with a string or rubber band. Set cans in a large pot on top of a baking rack, and fill the pot with boiling water to halfway up the cans. Cover pot and let the bread steam on low heat for 3 hours. (Time may be shortened by using a pressure cooker—follow instructions included with cooker.)

Makes 2 or 3 round loaves.

BANANA BREAD

½ cup milk
2 tsp. lemon juice
1 tsp. vanilla

¼ cup butter
⅓ cup honey
2 eggs
3 medium bananas, mashed
  (about 1½ cups)

1½ cups whole-wheat flour
1 cup rolled oats
2 tsp. soda
½ tsp. salt
½ tsp. cinnamon
½ cup chopped walnuts
1 cup finely chopped dates

Mix together the milk, lemon juice, and vanilla, and set aside.

Cream together the butter and honey, then mix in the eggs and bananas.

In a separate bowl combine the dry ingredients, including the walnuts and dates.

Add the dry ingredients to the butter mixture, along with the milk, and stir to mix.

Pour into 2 small greased and floured loaf pans and bake at 350° for 60 minutes, or until a toothpick inserted in the center comes out clean.

Makes 2 loaves.

CRANBERRY NUT BREAD

2 cups whole-wheat pastry flour
1½ tsp. baking powder
½ tsp. soda
½ tsp. salt

¼ cup butter

¾ cup orange juice
½ cup honey
1 egg, beaten
1 Tbsp. orange rind

½ cup chopped walnuts
1 cup whole cranberries

Mix together the dry ingredients. Cut in the butter until the mixture resembles coarse cornmeal.

Combine the orange juice, honey, egg, and orange rind. Pour into the dry ingredients, and mix just enough to dampen. Carefully fold in the nuts and cranberries.

Spoon into a greased and floured loaf pan, and bake at 350° for 1 hour—until the crust is golden brown and a toothpick comes out clean.

Makes 1 loaf.

CORN TORTILLAS

These are simple to make, but you must use masa—a special cornmeal ground with lime. Regular cornmeal won't do. Masa can often be found in the supermarket, near the cereals and flours.

> 2 cups masa harina
> 1¼ cups water

Mix the masa and water together with a spoon until you can knead it with your hands. Knead for 5 minutes, adding a bit of extra water, if necessary, to hold the dough together.

Form into smooth balls, about walnut-sized, then roll with a rolling pin on a floured board, or flatten with a tortilla press.

Cook in a hot, ungreased, cast iron skillet for 1½ minutes on each side, or until flecked with dark spots.

Makes 12 to 18 tortillas.

CHAPATIS (WHOLE-WHEAT TORTILLAS)

2 cups whole-wheat flour
½ tsp. salt
2 Tbsp. oil
½ cup water

Mix together the flour and salt, then add the oil and mix it in with your fingers or a fork until the mixture is homogeneous.

Stir in the water and work the dough in a bowl until it holds together easily. If the dough continues to crumble, add a little more water, 1 Tbsp. at a time, until the dough will hold together.

Take the dough out of the bowl and knead it on a lightly floured surface until it is smooth and elastic—about 5 minutes. Divide the dough into 10 equal-sized pieces and form each piece into a ball.

Roll the balls out on a well-floured surface into circles about 7 in. in diameter. Stack them and keep them covered to prevent them from drying out.

Heat a cast iron skillet or other heavy griddle. *Do not* butter or oil the pan. Cook the chapatis, one at a time, for a minute or two on each side. If they puff up, press them down gently with a spatula. They are done when light-brown spots show evenly on both sides.

Makes 10 chapatis.

CROUTONS

¼ cup butter
1½ tsp. dried parsley
1 clove garlic, minced
¼ tsp. thyme
⅛ tsp. oregano
⅛ tsp. basil
⅛ tsp. marjoram

about 8 slices bread

Mash butter until soft, then mix with the herbs.

Spread bread with the butter mixture, then stack the slices and cut into cubes. Spread the cubes out on a pie plate or other baking dish and bake at 300° until browned and crisp, about 20 minutes.

Makes 4 cups of croutons.

Entrees

VEGETABLE QUICHE

1 lb. spinach
2 Tbsp. olive oil
½ cup chopped green onions
  (tops included)
1 clove garlic, minced
1–2 cups sliced mushrooms
  (optional)
1½ cups (6 oz.) grated cheese
  (Cheddar, Jack, Swiss)
3 eggs, lightly beaten
¾ cup milk
1 tsp. crushed basil
¼ tsp. crushed celery seed
½ tsp. salt
1 9-in. whole-wheat pie crust, unbaked
  (see page 158)
2 medium tomatoes, thinly sliced
1 Tbsp. bread crumbs or wheat germ
1 Tbsp. Parmesan cheese

Steam the spinach until tender, chop fine, and drain.

Saute the onions and garlic in oil until the onions begin to color. If you are using mushrooms, saute them at this point. When they are lightly browned, add the spinach and cook over medium heat until excess liquid evaporates.

Mix together the cheese, eggs, milk, and herbs. Combine with the spinach mixture and blend well.

Pour into unbaked pie shell, and arrange the tomato slices around the top. Bake at 425° for 15 minutes. Lower temperature to 350° and bake 10 minutes longer.

Combine bread crumbs (or wheat germ) and Parmesan cheese. Sprinkle over tomatoes and bake 10 minutes more. (Quiche is done when the center moves only slightly.) Allow to stand a few minutes before cutting.

Serves 8.

SPINACH PIE

3 oz. cream cheese, softened
1 cup milk
½ cup soft bread cubes or crumbs
½ cup Parmesan cheese
2 eggs, beaten
2–3 Tbsp. butter
1 large onion, finely chopped
½ lb. mushrooms, finely chopped
1 cup cooked and drained spinach
1 tsp. tarragon
½ tsp. salt
1 9-in. whole-wheat pie crust,
   unbaked (page 158)

In a large bowl, mash the cream cheese; blend in the milk.

Add the bread cubes, Parmesan cheese, and eggs, and beat with a mixer or whisk to break up the bread.

Melt the butter in a large skillet and saute the onion and mushrooms until the onion is golden. Add the spinach and cook until the mixture is fairly dry.

Add the tarragon and salt, then stir the vegetables into the cheese mixture. Pour into unbaked pie shell and bake at 400° for 25 minutes.

Let stand 10 minutes before serving.

Serves 6 to 8.

NEAT LOAF

This incredibly high-protein dish has a look and texture similar to that of meat loaf (without the meat or the grease, however). It is great topped with catsup, and wonderful the next day when sliced for sandwiches.

> 1 cup cooked brown rice
> 2 cups shredded Cheddar cheese
> 1 cup wheat germ
> 1 cup chopped walnuts
> 1 cup chopped mushrooms
> 1 large onion, chopped
> ½ cup finely chopped green pepper
> ½ cup shredded carrot
> 4 eggs, lightly beaten
> 2 Tbsp. soy sauce
> 2 Tbsp. prepared mustard
> ½ tsp. thyme
> ½ tsp. marjoram
> ½ tsp. sage
>
> catsup

Combine all ingredients, and firmly pat into a greased 5 x 9-in. loaf pan.

Bake in a 350° oven for 55 minutes, or until lightly browned. You may top the loaf with catsup after 40 minutes, then return it to the oven to bake the remaining time.

Serves 8.

VEGIEBURGERS

2 stalks celery
2 carrots
1 onion
1 small head cauliflower
  or broccoli
2 medium zucchini
½ lb. mushrooms,
  chopped (2½ cups)
2 cloves garlic
2 Tbsp. parsley
1 cup sunflower seeds
4 Tbsp. olive oil

½ tsp. chili powder
½ tsp. cumin

½ tsp. curry powder
¼ tsp. sage
¼ tsp. red pepper
1 Tbsp. nutritional yeast
  (optional)
2 Tbsp. tamari soy
2 eggs, lightly beaten
½ cup cornmeal
¾ cup bread crumbs
1 cup rolled oats
2 cups cooked brown rice

thin slices Cheddar or Jack
  cheese

Chop finely or grate vegetables, garlic, parsley, and seeds.
  Cook in 2 Tbsp. olive oil over medium heat until soft and
fairly dry (about 20 minutes). Stir often.
  Remove from heat and stir in remaining ingredients
except cheese.
  Mix all ingredients well. Consistency should be firm
enough to form patties. If not, add more rolled oats.
  Form into patties and fry in 2 Tbsp. oil in a covered
skillet, until browned on bottom. Turn carefully and top
with slice of cheese.
  Cover pan and cook second side until cheese melts.
  Serve on a whole-wheat bun or on toasted whole-wheat
bread, with an assortment of garnishes, including lettuce,
red onion rings, tomatoes, or sprouts.
  Makes 12 to 16 patties.

BEANBURGERS

These are irresistibly delicious, and easy to assemble, once the beans and rice are cooked. I usually cook a large pot of beans, and another of rice, and keep the extra in the freezer, ready for the next time I want to make these.

1 cup cooked garbanzo beans,
    slightly ground
1 cup cooked brown rice
½ cup oatmeal, uncooked
1 tsp. paprika
2 Tbsp. soy sauce
¼ tsp. red pepper

1 stalk celery
1 small onion
1 clove garlic

butter for cooking
slices of cheese

Combine beans, rice, oatmeal, paprika, soy, and red pepper.

Chop finely and add celery, onion, and garlic.

Mix ingredients thoroughly and form into patties. Melt some butter in a skillet and cook patties on first side for 3 to 5 minutes, until browned.

Turn and top with a slice of cheese if desired, and cook until second side is brown.

Serve on buns, or topped with Mushroom Gravy (see page 75).

Makes 6 patties.

TOFU BURGERS

1 onion, chopped fine
1 cup finely chopped mushrooms
1 stalk celery, finely chopped
1 carrot, grated
½ bell pepper, grated
2 Tbsp. finely chopped fresh parsley
3 Tbsp. olive oil
1 lb. fresh tofu, mashed
2 eggs, lightly beaten
1 cup bread crumbs
½ cup rolled oats (more as needed)
½ tsp. salt
1 Tbsp. prepared mustard
2 tsp. cumin
½ tsp. curry powder
¼ tsp. red pepper

Sauté all vegetables, including parsley, in 1 Tbsp. oil until they are soft. Remove from heat.

Add remaining ingredients, and mix thoroughly. Add enough rolled oats to form a fairly stiff batter, from which patties can be formed.

Form patties, and fry, covered, in remaining oil. Serve with toasted bread or buns, and usual garnishes.

Serves 8.

BASIC CHEESE SOUFFLÉ

6 Tbsp. butter
6 Tbsp. whole-wheat flour
2 cups hot milk
½ tsp. salt
½ tsp. paprika
1 cup grated Cheddar cheese
6 eggs, separated
pinch cream of tartar (optional)

Melt the butter and stir in the flour; stir constantly over medium heat for about 2 minutes. Add the hot milk, and stir with a whisk until the sauce is quite thick. Add the seasonings and cheese, and stir until the cheese is all melted.

Remove the sauce from the heat and allow it to cool slightly.

Beat the eggs yolks, and whisk these into the cooled sauce.

Beat the egg whites, with a pinch of cream of tartar (optional) until they are stiff, but not dry.

Gently fold the beaten whites into the sauce, until the mixture is just homogeneous. Do not overmix, as you will lose too much air and the soufflé will not rise properly.

Pile the mixture into a greased 2-qt. souffle dish (the dish should be about ¾ full), and bake in a preheated 375° oven for 30 to 35 minutes, or until the top is golden brown and the soufflé is no longer wobbly.

Serve immediately!

Makes 6 servings.

CHEESY SCALLOPED POTATOES

The toasted sesame seeds make this a real treat.

⅔ cup sesame seeds, toasted
1 clove garlic, crushed
butter

8 medium potatoes
2 cups grated Cheddar cheese
2–3 Tbsp. butter
salt
paprika
1¼ cups hot milk

Toast sesame seeds by placing in a cast iron skillet over medium heat, for about 5 minutes. Stir occasionally.

Rub a 9 x 13-in. baking dish with the garlic, then butter it lightly.

Without peeling them, slice the potatoes very thin with a sharp knife or on the slicing side of a grater.

Place half the slices in the baking dish, then sprinkle with half the cheese and dot with half the butter. Sprinkle with half of the sesame seeds, then with salt and paprika.

Repeat the layers, then pour the hot milk over all.

Bake at 425° for 25 minutes, or until the potatoes are tender when pierced with a fork.

Serves 8.

SKILLET GREEN-BEAN PIE

Thanks to Mary Hordyke for this recipe.

1 lb. green beans, sliced
(French cut is nice, but not
absolutely necessary)
¼ cup chopped onion
2 Tbsp. oil

1 15-oz. can tomato sauce
2 Tbsp. sliced green onions
½ tsp. salt
6 eggs, beaten
1 cup shredded sharp Cheddar cheese (4 oz.)
2 Tbsp. chopped fresh parsley

Steam green beans until tender.

In large heavy skillet, sauté chopped onion in oil until tender. Add beans and tomato sauce. Cover and cook 5 minutes, stirring occasionally.

Meanwhile, add green onions and salt to eggs; set aside. Sprinkle cheese over beans in skillet; pour egg mixture on top. Cover and cook 10 minutes, or until eggs are firm. Remove from heat.

Uncover and let stand 10 minutes before serving. Sprinkle with parsley. Serve from skillet.

Serves 4.

ZUCCHINI CASSEROLE

My dear friend Carolyn Lynn, who insists she knows *nothing* about vegetarian cooking, gave me the recipe for this delicious casserole.

> 3 lb. zucchini, thinly sliced
> 1 red onion, finely chopped
> 2 Tbsp. butter or olive oil
> 4 oz. mild, green chiles, chopped
> 6 Tbsp. whole-wheat flour
> ¼ cup chopped fresh parsley
> ½ tsp. salt
> ¼ tsp. black pepper (optional)
> 3 cups grated Jack cheese
> 2 eggs, lightly beaten
> 2 cups cottage cheese
> 1 cup Parmesan cheese

Sauté the zucchini and the onion in the butter, and place in a large casserole.

Cover with the chiles, flour, parsley, salt, and pepper. Sprinkle the Jack cheese on top.

Mix the eggs and the cottage cheese in a bowl, and spoon evenly over the top of the casserole.

Sprinkle with Parmesan cheese and bake at 350° for 35 minutes.

Serves 8 to 10.

STUFFED EGGPLANT

3 small eggplants

2 bell peppers (red or green)
5 Tbsp. olive oil
1 tsp. salt

2 onions, chopped
2 cloves garlic, minced
3 Tbsp. finely chopped fresh parsley
1/4 tsp. basil
1 1/2 cups chopped tomatoes

2 Tbsp. butter
1/2 cup wheat germ
1/2 cup chopped walnuts
Parmesan cheese
   (approximately 1/4 cup)

Slice each eggplant in half lengthwise, and scoop out the insides, leaving a 1/4-in. layer in the skin. Set the shells aside.

Cut the insides into fairly large pieces, and dice the bell peppers into fairly small pieces. Sauté the eggplant and bell pepper in 3 Tbsp. olive oil, until the eggplant begins to soften. Season with salt and divide among the six eggplant shells, pressing it down.

Sauté the onion and garlic in the remaining 2 Tbsp. olive oil. When the onion is golden, add the parsley, basil, and tomatoes. Simmer 5 minutes, then spread on top of the eggplant mixture.

Melt the butter, then pour it over the wheat germ and chopped nuts. Stir to mix, then spread evenly over the six eggplant shells and pat it down. Sprinkle lightly with Parmesan cheese.

Bake in an oiled dish at 350° until shells are tender, about 45 minutes.

Serves 6.

BROWN RICE PIZZA

3 cups cooked brown rice
1 cup grated mozzarella cheese
½ cup sesame seeds
2 eggs, beaten

3 Tbsp. butter
3 Tbsp. whole-wheat flour
1½ cups milk
½ tsp. paprika

1 cup steamed broccoli
1 cup sliced and sautéed mushrooms
1 cup sautéed zucchini
2 tomatoes, sliced
½ lb. Muenster cheese, sliced
½ tsp. oregano

Allow rice to cool, then combine with mozzarella, sesame seeds, and eggs. Pat into a greased 12-in. pizza pan, and bake at 400° for 20 minutes.

To make the sauce, melt the butter, then add the flour and stir over medium heat for a minute. Whisk in the milk and paprika, then continue stirring over medium heat until sauce thickens. Spread sauce over baked crust.

Prepare vegetables as indicated. Arrange along with Muenster cheese, on top of pizza. Sprinkle with oregano.

Broil for 5 minutes, until cheese melts.

Serves 4 to 6.

RATATOUILLE

1 large eggplant, cubed

2 onions, chopped
3 Tbsp. olive oil
2 cloves garlic, crushed
2 medium potatoes, cubed
1 large bell pepper, diced
2 medium zucchini, thickly sliced

1 28-oz. can tomatoes
1½ tsp. basil
1 tsp. dill weed
½ tsp. oregano

2 cups cooked navy beans (optional)

Parmesan cheese

Cut the unpeeled eggplant into 1-in. cubes and set aside.

Chop the onion, and sauté it in the oil until it begins to turn golden. Add the garlic, potatoes, eggplant, bell pepper, and zucchini, and sauté over medium heat, stirring often, for 5 minutes. If the vegetables stick, a *small* amount of additional oil may be added.

Add the tomatoes and herbs, then cover and simmer until the eggplant and potatoes are tender, about 20 minutes. Add the cooked beans, if you are using them, and continue to simmer another 10 minutes.

Sprinkle with Parmesan cheese, and serve with brown rice.

Serves 8 to 10.

CORN PONE

This bean casserole has a moist, custardy cornbread on the top.

> 5-6 cups very juicy cooked
>   and seasoned beans (try
>   Chili Beans, page 116)
> 2 cups cornmeal
> 2 tsp. baking soda
> 1 tsp. salt
> 4 cups buttermilk, or 4 cups
>   milk + 4 Tbsp. vinegar or
>   lemon juice
> 2 eggs, lightly beaten
> ¼ cup melted butter or oil

Heat beans until they are quite hot, and pour into a large (at least 9 x 13-in.) baking dish.

Mix dry ingredients in a large bowl, and combine wet ingredients in another bowl.

Add wet ingredients to the dry, and stir together briefly. Pour the mixture over the hot beans, and bake in a preheated 400° oven until the bread is golden brown—30 minutes. *Note:* If you use milk and vinegar, the baking time may be longer, up to 50 minutes.

Serves 8.

PEANUT SPAGHETTI

This spaghetti casserole was the daring contribution to a class potluck, by a great lady named Alberta Foster. It is quite different, surprisingly tasty, and almost always a hit with children. I include the recipe for the adventurous, and for peanut lovers.

1 small onion, chopped
3 Tbsp. butter
4 Tbsp. whole-wheat flour
2 cups milk
½ tsp. salt
1 tsp. dry mustard
pinch cayenne

½ lb. whole-wheat spaghetti
½ cup sliced black olives
1 cup grated Cheddar cheese
1⅓ cup finely chopped peanuts

To prepare the sauce: Sauté the onion in the butter until it turns golden. Add the flour and stir for a minute or two. Whisk in the milk and seasonings, and stir until the sauce is thickened.

Break the spaghetti into manageable lengths, and cook it in boiling water until tender, about 10 minutes. Drain.

To assemble: Place half of the spaghetti in a greased casserole (approximately 8 x 11-in.), and top with half of the olives and cheese. Sprinkle ⅓ of the peanuts over this.

Repeat layers. Pour sauce over top. Sprinkle top with remaining peanuts.

Bake at 350° for 25 minutes.

Serves 6.

WONDERFUL CROCK-POT LENTILS

1¾ cups lentils, rinsed
2 large onions, chopped
2 cloves garlic, minced
2 cups canned tomatoes, chopped, with liquid
2 cups water or stock
2 large carrots, sliced
½ cup sliced celery
1 bell pepper, diced
2 Tbsp. chopped parsley
1 bay leaf
½ tsp. salt
⅛ tsp. marjoram
⅛ tsp. sage
⅛ tsp. thyme

½ lb. Cheddar cheese, shredded

Place all ingredients, except the cheese, in the crock pot and cook on the high setting for 2½ hours, or until the lentils are tender.

Stir in the cheese until it is melted, and serve.
Serves 8 to 10.

Note: This dish could also be made on the stove, using a heavy kettle and very low heat. Stir occasionally to prevent sticking or burning.

CROCK-POT SOYBEAN STEW

1 cup soybeans
4 cups water

1 onion, chopped
1 carrot, sliced
2 cloves garlic, minced
1 bay leaf
1 tsp. basil
2 Tbsp. soy sauce

2 cups Basic Tomato Sauce
(page 163), heated

Soak the soybeans in the 4 cups of water overnight, then cook them on high heat until they are tender, about 3 hours.

When the soybeans are fairly tender, add the onion, carrot, garlic, bay leaf, basil, and soy sauce. Cover and continue cooking on high for at least 3 hours.

Half an hour before eating, add the heated tomato sauce and cook until you are ready to eat.

Serve over polenta, whole-wheat pasta, or brown rice. Serves 6.

Note: To make this on the stove, simply cover and simmer on low heat for the same amounts of time as above. Check occasionally to be sure there is adequate liquid.

ZUCCHINI PIZZAS

This is a great way to use zucchini, easy to do and delicious.

> 4 small zucchini
> 1 Tbsp. olive oil
> 1 Tbsp. tamari soy sauce
> 1 tomato, chopped
> pinch of basil and oregano
> ½ cup grated Cheddar cheese
>
> pocket bread

Slice the zucchini into thin rounds, and sauté in the oil until they just begin to soften.

Add the tamari, tomatoes, and herbs and mix well. Sprinkle grated cheese on top, remove pan from heat, and cover until cheese is melted.

Stuff into pocket bread which has been warmed and cut in half.

This mixture will stuff about 6 pockets.

DEEP-DISH PIZZA

CRUST:

1 Tbsp. active dry yeast	*1 tsp. oregano*
1¾ cups warm water (about 110°)	*1 tsp. savory*
3 Tbsp. oil	*½ cup wheat germ*
1 tsp. salt	*2½ cups whole-wheat flour*
½ tsp. garlic powder	*2¼ cups unbleached or*
1 tsp. basil	*whole-wheat pastry flour*

To make the crust: Dissolve the yeast in ¼ cup of the warm water and let stand until bubbly.

Mix together the remaining water, the oil, salt, garlic, herbs, wheat germ, and whole-wheat flour. Add the yeast when it is bubbly, and beat until mixture is smooth and stretchy, about 5 minutes.

Gradually beat in the unbleached or pastry flour to form a moderately stiff dough. Turn onto a floured board and knead until smooth, about 8 minutes, adding flour as needed.

Turn in a greased bowl, cover, and let rise in a warm place until the size of the dough has doubled, about 1 hour.

Punch down and divide dough in half. Pat and stretch each half to cover the bottom and sides of a well-greased 9 x 13-in. baking dish.

(Or make Quick Crust—see below.)

QUICK CRUST:

2 cups whole-wheat flour	*1 tsp. oregano*
2 tsp. baking powder	*1 tsp. savory*
½ tsp. salt	*¼ cup oil*
½ tsp. garlic powder	*⅔ cup water*
1 tsp. basil	

Mix dry ingredients, then cut in oil until mixture resembles fine cornmeal.

Add water, stirring as you do so, until mixture leaves side of bowl. Gather dough into a ball, then knead 10 times to make smooth. Divide dough in half, then work each half into a greased 9 x 13-in. baking dish.

SAUCE:

2 large onions, chopped
2 cloves garlic, minced
2 Tbsp. olive oil
1 15-oz. can tomato sauce

1 6-oz. can tomato paste
1 tsp. oregano
1 tsp. basil
½ tsp. salt

Sauté the onion and garlic in the oil until the onion turns golden. Stir in the remaining ingredients and simmer, uncovered, for 10 minutes.

TOPPING:

2 cups (½ lb.) mozzarella, Jack, Cheddar, or Swiss cheese
½ cup grated Parmesan cheese

Any combination of the following:
1 large onion, chopped
1 large bell pepper, chopped
1½ lbs. mushrooms, sliced and sautéed in 2 Tbsp. butter
1½ cups sliced olives
2 large, ripe tomatoes, sliced

To assemble: Divide sauce between the 2 baked crusts, and spread evenly. Sprinkle half the cheese over each pizza, and top with any of the suggested toppings. Sprinkle Parmesan cheese over all, and bake at 400° for 25 minutes.
   Makes 2 9 x 13-in. pizzas.

STUFFED CHARD OR CABBAGE LEAVES

1½ cups brown rice
3 cups water
½ tsp. salt

SAUCE:
½ cup chopped onion
1 Tbsp. olive oil
2 cups chopped tomatoes

FILLING:
2 cups chopped onion
2 cloves garlic, minced
2 Tbsp. butter
1 lb. mushrooms, sliced (4 cups)
.1 tsp. paprika
⅛ tsp. cayenne
¾ cup raisins
¾ cup chopped walnuts
2 eggs, lightly beaten
½ cup whole-wheat bread crumbs

16–20 chard or cabbage leaves

¼ lb. Feta cheese, crumbled

Begin cooking the rice: Bring the water to a boil, then add ½ tsp. salt and the rice. When the water boils again, cover the pan, lower the heat, and simmer 40 to 50 minutes, until the rice is done.

While the rice is cooking, prepare the sauce: Chop the onion and saute it in the olive oil until it is golden. Add the tomatoes, coarsely chopped, stir thoroughly, and heat through.

Now prepare the filling: Saute the onions and garlic in the butter until the onions are golden. Add the mushrooms and cook lightly.

Add the cooked rice, along with all the remaining ingredients except the chard and the cheese and cook over low heat until dry.

Lightly steam the chard or cabbage leaves until they are soft enough to roll.

Place a generous spoonful of the filling onto each leaf, sprinkle with some crumbled cheese, and roll the leaf up, tucking in the sides as you go. Place the rolled leaves in a baking dish that has 1 cup of the sauce spread over the bottom of it, and *lightly* cover with the sauce.

Bake at 350° for 20 minutes.

Serves 8 to 10.

LASAGNA

*3 cups Basic Tomato Sauce
(see page 163)
½ lb. whole-wheat lasagna noodles
½ lb. fresh spinach or 1 pkg.
frozen, thawed
½ cup chopped nuts: walnuts,
almonds, sunflower seeds
2 cups cottage cheese or
ricotta cheese
½–1 cup grated Parmesan cheese
½ lb. mozzarella cheese,
grated (about 2½ cups)*

Begin the tomato sauce. While it is simmering, prepare the remaining ingredients.

Cook the noodles in boiling water until tender (about 15 minutes) and drain.

Pick over and wash the spinach well, then chop it into bite-sized pieces.

To assemble: Spread ¾ cup of sauce in the bottom of a 9 x 13-in. baking dish. Place ¾ of the noodles over this, and cover with ¾ of the spinach, nuts, cottage cheese, Parmesan, and mozzarella.

Repeat layers twice. Pour remaining sauce over all and sprinkle with Parmesan.

Bake at 350° for 40 minutes. Let stand 10 minutes before serving.

Serves 8.

great Italian lady named Olympia first made this for me, and it's been one of my favorites since.

> 1 recipe Basic Tomato Sauce
>   (see page 163)
> 2 cups sliced mushrooms
>
> 1 cup polenta (coarse-ground cornmeal)
> 1 cup cold water
> ½–1 tsp. salt
> 4 cups boiling water
> Parmesan cheese, grated

Prepare the Basic Tomato Sauce, adding the mushrooms when you saute the onion.

To cook the polenta: Mix the polenta with 1 cup cold water and the salt, then add it to the 4 cups of boiling water, stirring constantly. Cover and cook it for 25 minutes, stirring frequently.

Top the cooked polenta with a generous portion of the Tomato Sauce, and sprinkle it with Parmesan cheese.

Serves 6 to 8.

Variation: Try polenta topped with Soybean Stew (page 106)

EGGPLANT PARMESAN

*3 cups Basic Tomato Sauce
  (page 163)
1 cup sesame seeds, toasted
½ cup Parmesan cheese, grated*

*1 large eggplant
½ lb. mozzarella cheese, grated*

Prepare the tomato sauce as directed. Toast the sesame seeds by heating them in a heavy skillet over medium heat for about 5 minutes. When the sauce is ready, stir in the sesame seeds and the Parmesan cheese.

Without peeling it, slice the eggplant into ½-in.-thick rounds. Place it on an oiled cookie sheet, and bake it at 350° for 20 minutes, or until tender when pierced with a fork. (*Note:* It is important that the eggplant be quite tender. Chewy eggplant is *not* pleasant.)

To assemble: Place a layer of eggplant in a greased 9 x 13-in. baking dish. Cover it with half the tomato sauce, then half the mozzarella cheese. Repeat the layers, and sprinkle with Parmesan cheese.

Bake at 350° for 30 minutes.

Serves 6 to 8.

EGGPLANT CANNELLONI

This is a delicious and elegant dish—especially when prepared in individual casseroles. I usually reserve it for special occasions, as it takes 2 to 3 hours to prepare.

1 large eggplant

SAUCE:
2 Tbsp. olive oil
1 small onion, chopped
2 cloves garlic, crushed
½ bell pepper, chopped
1 Tbsp. chopped fresh parsley
¼ tsp. oregano
¼ tsp. basil
4 cups tomatoes, well
    chopped
1 small bay leaf
¼ tsp. salt
1 slice lemon peel
½ cup red wine

FILLING:
2 eggs, lightly beaten
1 cup ricotta or cottage
    cheese, blended smooth
½ cup grated Parmesan
    cheese
2 cups shredded mozzarella or
    Jack cheese
¼ tsp. nutmeg
⅛ tsp. black pepper
1 Tbsp. chopped fresh parsley

BATTER:
1 egg, lightly beaten
⅔ cup milk
4 Tbsp. whole-wheat flour

TO BAKE:
whole-wheat flour
pumpkin seeds
Parmesan cheese

Slice the eggplant *lengthwise* into 12 equally thick (about ½-in.) slices. Place on a rack to drain for ½ hour.

While the eggplant drains, begin the sauce: Sauté the onion, garlic, and bell pepper in the oil until the onion is golden, then add the herbs and cook briefly. Add the tomatoes, bay leaf, salt, and lemon peel. Allow the sauce to simmer gently for at least ½ hour. Add the wine for the last 15 minutes.

Combine the filling ingredients, and blend well. Set aside.

Press each piece of eggplant with a dry towel, then combine the ingredients for the batter. Coat each slice of eggplant with flour, then dip in batter on one side and place on an oiled sheet, batter side up. Bake in a 350° oven 20 to 30 minutes, until tender when pierced with a fork.

When the eggplant is cool enough to handle, place a spoonful of filling across the center (unbattered side) of each slice. Fold the narrow end over the filling, and roll closed. Arrange, seam side down, in a casserole dish, or in 6 individual casseroles.

Sprinkle a few pumpkin seeds over each cannelloni, then spoon sauce over all. Top with grated Parmesan, and bake uncovered at 375° for 15 to 20 minutes.

Serves 6.

MEXICAN RICE BREAD

1 cup cornmeal
½ tsp. salt
½ tsp. soda

1 cup milk
2 eggs, beaten
2 Tbsp. melted butter
2 cups cooked brown rice
1 pkg. frozen corn, thawed, or
    1 can creamed corn
1 small onion, chopped
4 Tbsp. mild, green chiles, diced
½ lb. Cheddar cheese (2½ cups, grated)

Mix together the cornmeal, salt, and soda. Add remaining ingredients and stir to blend.

Pour into a 12-in. skillet which has been greased, and bake at 350° for 45 minutes.

Serves 8.

CHILI BEANS

3 cups dried pinto beans*
8–9 cups water
4 cloves garlic, minced
¾ tsp. cumin

2 onions, chopped
2 bell peppers, chopped
2 Tbsp. olive oil
4 cups (2 15-oz. cans) tomato sauce
2 cups corn, fresh or frozen
1 tsp. salt
½ tsp. oregano
1½ tsp. chili powder (or more to taste)
⅛ tsp. cayenne (or more to taste)

Cook the beans in the water, along with the garlic and cumin, until they are tender—about 3 hours. (You may soak the beans overnight, prior to cooking them, if you wish. This will cut their cooking time by about ½ hour.)

Sauté the onion and pepper in the olive oil until the onion turns golden. Add to the cooked beans, along with the remaining ingredients, and simmer at least 30 minutes. Serves 8 to 10.

Note: This is a perfect recipe for the crock pot. Begin cooking the beans in the morning. If you start with hot water and use the high setting, they will take 3 to 4 hours to cook. Add the remaining ingredients in the late afternoon, and continue cooking until dinnertime.

*3 cups dried beans will make about 7 cups cooked beans.

REFRIED BEANS I

1½ cups dry pinto beans
4 cups water
2 cloves garlic, minced
1 tsp. cumin
⅓ tsp. cayenne

1 onion, chopped
2 cloves garlic, minced
¼ cup olive oil
1 cup chopped tomatoes
3 Tbsp. diced mild, green chiles

1–2 tsp. salt
2 Tbsp. butter (optional)

Simmer the beans, along with the garlic, cumin, and cayenne, for 3 hours, or until tender.

In a large skillet, sauté the onion and garlic in olive oil until the onion is golden. Stir in the tomatoes and chiles, then begin adding the beans, a cup at a time, and mashing them. When all the beans have been added, stir to mix, then cook over low heat, stirring frequently, until the mixture is quite thick. Add salt to taste, and the butter if desired.

Serves 8.

REFRIED BEANS II

These are absolutely the best refried beans I have ever eaten. Their flavor is somewhat different from the typical cumin-flavored beans you're used to, but don't let that deter you.

It is best, but not essential, to soak the beans overnight. If you forget, don't let this stop you from making these wonderful, spicy beans. Just allow an extra half hour for the beans to cook.

1½ cups dried pinto beans
5–6 cups water
1½ onions
¼ cup olive oil
3–4 cloves garlic, minced
1 cup chopped tomatoes,
    fresh or canned
¼ cup diced mild, green chiles
    (or more to taste)

2 Tbsp. lemon juice
2 tsp. salt
¼ tsp. cinnamon
⅛ tsp. cloves

grated Jack cheese (about 1 cup)

Pick any foreign objects out of the beans and rinse well. Place in a large pot with the water. Chop half an onion and add it to the beans. Cover and bring to a simmer. Cook 2½ to 3 hours, until the beans are tender. (Be sure to check occasionally to be sure there is adequate liquid.)

When the beans are tender, heat the olive oil in a very large skillet. Chop the remaining onion, and sauté it, with the minced garlic, until it is golden. Add the tomatoes, peppers, lemon juice, salt, and spices. Stir to mix.

Begin adding the beans, with their liquid, a cup at a time, and mash. (I prefer to leave some of the beans unmashed.) Stir to mix, then cook the beans over low heat, stirring frequently, until the mixture is quite thick; this may take an hour or more.

When the beans are thick, stir the cheese into them, or pour them into a casserole and top with the cheese.

Serves 6 to 8.

EGGPLANT ENCHILADAS

1 batch Enchilada Sauce (see page 121)

1 onion, chopped
2 Tbsp. olive oil
2 cloves garlic, minced
1 medium eggplant, cubed
1 bell pepper, diced
1 tsp. salt
1 tsp. red pepper
1 cup chopped walnuts
1½ cups grated Jack cheese

1 dozen tortillas

Prepare the enchilada sauce.

While the sauce simmers, sauté the onion in the 2 Tbsp. oil until it turns golden. Add the garlic and the eggplant, and toss to coat with oil. Cover and cook over medium heat until the eggplant is soft, about 10 minutes.

Add bell pepper, seasonings, and walnuts, and cook 5 more minutes. Remove from heat and stir in 1 cup of cheese.

To assemble: Soften tortillas by placing them, one at a time, in the hot enchilada sauce for about 30 seconds. Fill with about ¼ cup of the eggplant mixture, and roll tightly. Place in a large baking dish, or into individual casseroles. When all the tortillas have been filled, pour hot sauce over the top and sprinkle with remaining grated cheese.

Bake at 350° for 20 minutes.

Serves 6.

SPANISH RICE

1 onion, chopped
1 bell pepper, diced
2 cloves garlic, minced
2 Tbsp. oil
4 cups cooked brown rice,
   well chilled
1 tsp. tamari soy
2 tsp. chili powder

Be sure the rice is very cold, or it will stick.

Sauté the onion, bell pepper, and garlic in the oil. When the onion is golden, add the rice, soy sauce, and chili powder. Cook, stirring often, over medium heat, until the rice is very hot.

Serves 6 to 8.

CHEESE ENCHILADAS

1 medium onion, chopped
3 cloves garlic, minced
2 Tbsp. olive oil
¼ cup Ortega mild, green chiles
    (or more to taste)
4 cups chopped tomatoes,
    fresh or cannned
¼ tsp. oregano
¼ tsp. basil
¼ tsp. cumin

2½ cups sharp Cheddar
    cheese or 1¼ cups Cheddar
    and 1½ cups cottage cheese
¾ cup black olives
½ cup green onions
1 Tbsp. chopped parsley

12 corn tortillas

Prepare the sauce first: Saute the onion and garlic in the oil until the onion is golden.

Add the chiles, tomatoes, and herbs. Simmer over low heat for at least 15 minutes. If the sauce becomes too thick, you may add a bit of water.

While the sauce simmers, prepare the filling: Grate the cheese and place in a bowl. Slice the olives, chop the green onions and parsley, and place each in a separate bowl.

To assemble: Spread ½ cup of the sauce in the bottom of a casserole (approximately 9 x 13-in.). Place a tortilla in the hot sauce until soft. Remove it gently, then fill it with approximately 3 Tbsp. cheese (or cheese and cottage cheese), and a sprinkling of olives, green onions, and parsley. Roll the tortilla around the filling, and place in the baking dish, seam side down. Repeat with remaining tortillas.

When all the tortillas are finished, pour the sauce over all, and bake at 350° for 15 to 20 minutes.

Serves 8.

TOFU TORTILLA CASSEROLE

This delicious casserole is a wonderful way to introduce skeptics to tofu. The original recipe calls for sour cream, but I've used ricotta cheese, or cottage cheese blended smooth, with equally tasty results.

> 1 medium onion, chopped
> 2 cloves garlic, minced
> 1 lb. tofu, mashed
> 2 Tbsp. olive oil
> 1 28-oz. can tomatoes,
>   chopped, with liquid
> 3 Tbsp. chili powder
> 1½ tsp. cumin
> 1 tsp. salt
> 10 tortillas, torn into sixths
> ½ lb. Cheddar cheese, grated
>   (2½ cups)
> 1½ cups chopped green onions
> 1 pint cottage cheese, blended smooth
> 1 cup black olives, chopped or sliced

Saute the onion, garlic, and tofu in the olive oil.

Add tomatoes with their liquid, and the seasonings, and simmer for 20 minutes.

To assemble: Spread ½ cup of sauce on the bottom of a large casserole. Cover with half the tortilla pieces, then ¾ of the grated cheese, chopped onion, cottage cheese, and chopped olives. Repeat once, then end with a layer of sauce, dollops of cottage cheese, and a sprinkling of green onions and olives.

Bake at 350° for 20 minutes.

Serves 8.

TOFU-STUFFED SHELLS

1 medium onion, chopped
3 cloves garlic, minced
1 Tbsp. olive oil
½ tsp. basil
½ tsp. oregano
¼ tsp. thyme
1 small carrot, grated
1 28-oz. can tomatoes,
   chopped, with liquid

24 whole-wheat macaroni
   shells

1 lb. tofu, mashed
2 Tbsp. chopped fresh parsley
½ tsp. basil
½ tsp. oregano
½ tsp. salt
1 egg, lightly beaten
1 10-oz. pkg. frozen spinach,
   thawed, or 10 oz. fresh
   spinach, cooked
⅓ cup grated Parmesan
   cheese

For sauce: Sauté onion and garlic in oil until onion is golden. Remove half the onion and set aside for the filling.

Add spices, carrot, and tomatoes, and simmer for 20 minutes or more.

Cook whole-wheat shells in boiling water for 3 minutes, until they are just getting tender. Drain and cool.

Mash the tofu, and mix with all the remaining ingredients except the Parmesan, including the sautéed onion which has been set aside.

To assemble: Stuff the shells with the tofu mixture, and place in a 9 x 13-in. dish which has ½ cup of sauce spread in the bottom of it. Spoon remaining sauce over all, and sprinkle with Parmesan.

Cover with foil and bake in a 350° oven for 30 minutes. At the end of the baking time, pierce a shell or two with a fork to make sure they are tender. If not, cover and bake 10 minutes longer. Serve immediately.

Serves 8 to 10.

Note: 12 manicotti shells may be used in place of the whole-wheat shells. Procedure is the same.

FRIED TOFU

1 lb. fresh tofu
2–3 Tbsp. oil
1–2 Tbsp. soy sauce

Wrap tofu in a clean dish towel, and press gently to remove excess moisture. Cut tofu into thin chunks, about ¾ x ¾ x ¼-in.

Heat oil in a heavy skillet, and add tofu. Fry over medium heat until tofu is well browned. This will take 5 to 10 minutes. Sprinkle soy sauce over tofu, and toss to coat all pieces evenly.

Serve hot with Mushroom Gravy (see page 75), catsup, or plain.

Serves 4.

TOFU LASAGNA

3 Tbsp. butter
½ lb. mushrooms, thinly sliced
3 cloves garlic, finely chopped
½ tsp. salt
3 cups Basic Tomato Sauce
  (page 163)
½ cup wheat germ
1 cup mashed tofu
¼ cup grated Parmesan cheese
½ lb. mozzarella cheese,
  grated (about 2½ cups)
¼ cup chopped fresh parsley
8 oz. lasgana noodles, cooked
  and drained

Melt butter in a large skillet, and sauté mushrooms and garlic until mushrooms are tender—about 5 minutes. Add salt, Tomato Sauce, and wheat germ, and heat.

Combine tofu and Parmesan cheese; in another bowl, combine mozzarella and parsley.

Place ⅓ of the cooked noodles in the bottom of a 9 x 13-in. baking dish. Spread half of the tofu mixture on top; pour ⅓ of the sauce over the tofu and top this with ⅓ of the mozzarella. Repeat this layering, then make a final layer of noodles, sauce, and mozzarella mixture.

Bake at 350° for 45 minutes, or until hot and bubbly. Let stand 10 minutes before cutting.

Serves 8.

MOUSSAKA

1 cup lentils, uncooked
3 cups water

1 large eggplant

3 Tbsp. olive oil
2 large onions, chopped
1 clove garlic, minced
¾ tsp. oregano
1½ tsp. cinnamon
1 tsp. salt

1 28-oz. can tomatoes,
  chopped (4 cups), with
  liquid
6 oz. tomato paste
7 oz. whole-wheat lasagna
  noodles
3 cups milk
3 Tbsp. butter
6 Tbsp. whole-wheat flour
½–1 cup grated Parmesan
  cheese

Wash the lentils, cover them with 3 cups of water, and bring to a boil. Reduce heat, and simmer until tender, not mushy—about 1 hour.

Chop the eggplant (unpeeled) into medium-sized (about ½-in.) cubes, and set aside for at least ½ hour. At the end of this time, press out the excess moisture with a clean dish towel.

Heat olive oil in a large skillet and add the chopped onions. Sauté until the onion is just golden, then add the garlic and other seasonings and mix thoroughly.

Add the eggplant and sauté, stirring often, about 5 minutes.

Add the tomatoes, along with their liquid, and the tomato paste. Add the lentils, and cook until the mixture is thick and the eggplant is tender.

In the meantime, prepare the lasagna noodles. Cook them in boiling water until they are tender—about 10 to 12 minutes.

Prepare a white sauce: Begin heating the milk in a saucepan. In another saucepan, melt the butter. Stir in the flour and let the mixture cook a few minutes, stirring often. Pour in the heated milk, stirring constantly with a whisk to keep it smooth. Cook over low heat, stirring constantly, until mixture starts to thicken—about 5 minutes.

Butter a large casserole and place a layer of noodles (⅓ of the noodles) across the bottom.

Cover them with ⅓ of the lentil-eggplant mixture. Top

this with about ¼ cup of Parmesan cheese and ⅓ of the white sauce.

Repeat these layers twice again, ending with a sprinkling of Parmesan on the very top.

Bake at 375° for 1 hour.

Serves 8.

FEIJOADA (TANGY BLACK BEANS)

This is a traditional Brazilian dish, and is typically served with Spanish (Brazilian?) rice and hot sauce.

> 2 cups dry black beans
> 6 cups water or stock (wine may
>   be substituted, up to 1 cup)
>
> 2 large onions, chopped
> 1 clove garlic, minced
> 2 Tbsp. olive oil
>
> 1 bay leaf
> 1 orange, halved
> 1 tsp. salt
> 4 stalks celery, chopped
> 2 cups chopped tomatoes

Wash the beans thoroughly. Place them in a kettle with the water or stock, bring to a boil, then reduce heat and simmer.

Sauté the onion and garlic in the oil and add them to the uncooked beans.

Add the remaining ingredients and simmer until the beans are tender (about 3 hours). Remove the bay leaf and orange, and serve hot with rice.

Serves 8.

MJEDDRAH

This is a very old dish from the Middle East. According to biblical scholars, Mjeddrah is the "mess of pottage" for which Esau sold his birthright to Jacob, and when you taste its simple hearty flavor, I think you'll see why.

1½ cups lentils
4 cups cold water
2 large onions
3 Tbsp. olive oil

2 tsp. salt
1½ Tbsp. butter
¾ cup brown rice

Rinse the lentils and place them in a pot with the 4 cups of cold water. Bring to a boil over medium heat, then reduce to a simmer and cover tightly.

Chop the onions coarsely, then saute them in the olive oil until they are golden. Stir in 1 tsp. salt, then add the onions to the lentils.

Melt the butter, then saute the rice until it just starts to brown (about 3 minutes). Add the rice, along with the remaining salt, to the lentils.

Cover tightly and simmer until the rice and lentils are tender (about 1 hour). Additional water—up to 2 cups—may be added, if necessary, to cook the rice.

Be sure and stir occasionally, toward the end, to prevent sticking.

Mjeddrah is traditionally eaten with the following salad on top of it.

lettuce
spinach
tomatoes
green onions
cucumber
radishes
bell pepper
sprouts
Feta cheese, crumbled

DRESSING:
3 Tbsp. olive oil
2 Tbsp. lemon juice
½ tsp. paprika
¼ tsp. dry mustard
1 clove garlic, minced
¼ tsp. salt
¼ tsp. honey

Serves 6 to 8.

FALAFEL (MIDDLE EASTERN TACO)

1 cup dry garbanzo beans
  (chick peas)
4 cups water

½ cup (heaping) sesame seeds
¼ cup finely chopped parsley
1 tsp. coriander, ground
¾ tsp. cumin, ground
½ tsp. salt
⅛ tsp. cayenne
3 cloves garlic, minced
2 Tbsp. lemon juice

2-4 Tbsp. olive oil for frying
1 package pocket bread

POSSIBLE GARNISHES:
lettuce, shredded
alfalfa sprouts
tomatoes, chopped
cucumber, sliced
green onion, chopped

yogurt or sour cream

Rinse the garbanzos thoroughly, and soak in 4 cups of water overnight. (This cuts cooking time by 30 minutes—can be omitted.) Cover and simmer about 3 hours, until the beans are quite tender.

Mash the beans coarsely, and add the seasonings and lemon juice. Mix well and let stand at least ½ hour at room temperature.

Just before you are ready to eat, pour the olive oil into a large skillet. Add the garbanzo mixture, and cook until very hot.

Steam the pocket bread lightly, or place in the oven, until soft and warm. Cut each piece in half, and fill the pockets with about ¼ cup of the bean mixture.

Garnish with lettuce, sprouts, tomato, cucumber; or green onion, and top with yogurt or sour cream.

Serves 6.

VEGETABLE CURRY

This recipe is great for newcomers to curry, since it is fairly mild. It is quite easy to prepare if you do all the slicing, chopping, and mincing before you start cooking.

6 Tbsp. oil
1 large onion
1 Tbsp. fresh ginger
2 cloves garlic
1 Tbsp. curry powder
1½ tsp. salt
½ tsp. cumin
½ tsp. coriander
⅛–¼ tsp. cayenne

2 large tomatoes
2 medium carrots
½ lb. mushrooms
4 medium-sized zucchini
1 green bell pepper
1 red bell pepper (optional)
1½ cups cooked garbanzo
    beans (chick peas)
1 cup plain yogurt

Begin by preparing the vegetables:
Thinly slice the onion.
Mince the ginger and the garlic, very fine.
Cut the tomatoes into ½-in. wedges.
Slice the carrots thinly.
Slice the mushrooms.
Cut the zucchini into ½-in. thick slices.
Cut the pepper(s) into thin strips.

Put the oil in a heavy skillet or Dutch oven and place over medium-low heat. Saute the onion and ginger until the onion is golden. Add the garlic, salt, spices, and tomatoes. Stir gently to mix.

Add the carrots, mushrooms, zucchini, and peppers. Cover and cook, over medium-low heat, 10 to 15 minutes, until the carrots are just getting tender.

Just before the vegetables are done (after about 10 minutes), add the cooked, drained garbanzo beans. Cook until the beans are hot, about 5 minutes.

Remove the pan from the heat, and stir in the yogurt. Serve immediately. (If you must heat or reheat this dish, do so only over *very low heat,* as the yogurt will curdle if it gets too hot and boils.)

Serve with peanuts, raisins, other dried fruits, coconut, chutney, and any other condiments of your choosing.

Serves 6 to 8.

DAL

Dal is popular in many areas in India, and provides one of the most concentrated sources of protein in the Indian diet. There are innumerable variations on the basic recipe which follows.

> 1½ cups yellow split peas
> 1 tsp. salt
> 4 cups water
>
> 3 Tbsp. butter
> 1 tsp. ground cumin
> 1 tsp. ground turmeric
> ½ tsp. cinnamon
> ⅛–¼ tsp. cayenne
> ¼ tsp. ground ginger
> ¼ tsp. ground coriander
> ½ tsp. mustard seeds

Wash the peas and place them in a kettle with the salt and the water. Cover and simmer until tender, about 1 hour.

Melt the butter in a skillet and add the spices to it. Stir them around for a few minutes, then remove the pan from the heat.

Pour in the cooked peas, being careful to protect yourself from the splattering that may occur. Return the pan to the heat and simmer, stirring often, until the dal is the consistency of a fairly thick sauce.

Serve very hot, with curried rice and a raita.

Serves 6.

CURRIED RICE

3 cups water
¾ tsp. salt
1½ cups brown rice

2 Tbsp. butter or oil
½ onion, chopped
1 large clove garlic, minced
½ bell pepper, chopped
½ cup raisins
2 tsp. curry powder (or more to taste)
¼ cup water
1 cup green peas, lightly cooked

Bring the water to a boil, then add the salt and the rice. Reduce heat, cover, and simmer for 40 minutes.

Just before the rice is done, melt the butter and sauté the onion until it begins to get golden. Add the garlic and the bell pepper, and sauté a couple more minutes.

Add the raisins, the curry powder, and ¼ cup of water, and stir over medium-low heat for 3 to 5 minutes—until the raisins are just getting soft. Remove from heat, and stir in the lightly cooked peas.

Add the curry mixture to the rice, stir together gently, and cook without stirring until the rice is done—about 5 more minutes.

Serves 6.

VEGETABLE SPAGHETTI

1 cup lentils
3 cups water
½ tsp. salt

2 onions, chopped
3 Tbsp. olive oil
2 cloves garlic, minced
1 large eggplant, cubed
1 large bell pepper, diced
2 medium zucchini, thickly sliced

2 15-oz. cans tomato sauce
1 6-oz. can tomato paste
1½ tsp. basil
1 tsp. oregano
½ tsp. dill weed
1 tsp. thyme

1 lb. spaghetti

Parmesan cheese

Rinse the lentils, then add them to the water, along with the salt, and simmer for 1 hour.

Sauté the onion in the oil until it is golden, then add the remaining vegetables and continue to cook over medium heat, stirring often, for 5 minutes.

Stir in the cooked lentils, tomato sauce, tomato paste, and herbs. Cover and simmer until the eggplant is tender, about 20 minutes.

Cook the spaghetti in boiling water until it is tender, then drain and mix with the vegetable sauce. Sprinkle liberally with Parmesan cheese and serve.

Serves 8 to 10.

CHINESE FRIED RICE

It is essential that the rice be quite cold so that it will not stick.

>3 cups water
>1½ cups long-grain brown rice
>5 green onions
>
>2 Tbsp. oil (peanut is most authentic)
>1 clove garlic, minced
>½ tsp. ginger root, minced
>2–3 Tbsp. tamari soy
>2 eggs (optional)

Bring the water to a boil and add the rice. Lower the heat, then cover and simmer 45 minutes, until the rice is tender and dry. Place rice in refrigerator and chill thoroughly.

Chop the green onions, keeping the white and green parts separate.

Sauté the white part of the onions in the oil, along with the garlic and the ginger root, until the onions are just turning golden. Add the rice and cook, stirring constantly, 2 to 3 minutes. Pour in the soy sauce to taste, and continue to cook until the mixture is thoroughly heated and well blended.

Stir in green part of scallions or onions, and the eggs (already cooked, see below), if you are using them. Stir thoroughly and serve.

If you are using eggs: Beat eggs with ½ tsp. soy sauce and 1 Tbsp. water. Heat 1 Tbsp. oil in a skillet, then pour in the eggs. Cook without stirring until just set. Remove from pan and cut into small pieces.

Serves 6.

TOFU/BROWN RICE CASSEROLE

CASSEROLE:
4 cups cooked brown rice
2 cups tofu, mashed or diced
1½ cups chopped green
  onions, including tops
½ cup diced bell pepper
1½ cups finely chopped celery
1½ cups grated Cheddar cheese
1 cup chopped walnuts
1 cup yogurt
1 tsp. salt
½–1 tsp. tarragon
pinch cayenne

TOPPING:
1½ cups bread crumbs
2–3 Tbsp. butter, melted
2 Tbsp. Parmesan cheese

Combine all casserole ingredients, mix well, then pat into a 9 x 12-in. baking dish.

Mix topping ingredients, and spread evenly over casserole.

·Bake at 350° for 20 minutes.

Serves 8.

Variations: Add 1 cup chopped olives, 1 cup raisins, or 2 cups finely chopped mushrooms. Or use the mixture to stuff your favorite vegetables: zucchini, eggplant, bell pepper.

VEGETABLES AND TOFU

This recipe is endlessly variable, depending on the season, your energy and tastes, and the vegetables in your garden or refrigerator. Try using different vegetables as they are in season.

The key to the success of this recipe is to cook the vegetables until they are *just tender;* most vegetables will become very brilliant in color at this point, after which their color will begin to fade.

> *1 lb. tofu*
>
> *4 cups cooked brown rice*
>
> *2–4 Tbsp. oil*
> *2 carrots*
> *2 stalks celery*
> *1 small onion*
> *1 tsp. fresh ginger root, very*
> * finely chopped*
> *1 clove garlic, minced*
> *1 bell pepper*
> *2 cups sliced mushrooms*
> * (approximately ½ lb.)*
> *2 medium zucchini*
>
> *3 Tbsp. tamari soy*
> *1 Tbsp. honey*
> *¼ cup sesame seeds*

First prepare the vegetables: Slice the carrots and celery on the diagonal, cut the onion and bell pepper into thin strips, slice the mushrooms, and slice the zucchini into thin rounds.

Dice the tofu into ½-in. cubes.

Place the cooked rice in a fairly large casserole dish in a 200° oven.

Pour 2 Tbsp. of oil in a large skillet or wok, and begin sautéeing the carrots. After a few minutes, add the celery, onion, ginger root, and garlic, and continue to cook over medium heat until the onion is golden.

Add the pepper, mushrooms, and zucchini, and cook,

stirring often, for 2 to 3 minutes. Add 1 Tbsp. of the soy sauce, then cover and cook until the vegetables are just tender, about 2 to 3 more minutes.

Spoon the vegetables over the rice, and return the casserole to the oven.

Add 2 Tbsp. oil to the skillet, and sauté the tofu until it is lightly browned. Add the remaining soy sauce and honey, and stir the tofu to coat it. Place the tofu on top of the vegetables, sprinkle with the sesame seeds, and serve immediately.

Serves 6 to 8.

BROCCOLI TOFU PIE

1½ lbs. broccoli
1 medium onion, chopped
4 Tbsp. butter or oil
2 Tbsp. flour
1½ Tbsp. miso or ½ tsp. salt
¾ cup water or stock
½ lb. tofu, drained and mashed
½ cup grated Cheddar cheese
½ cup sunflower seeds
2 Tbsp. sesame seeds, toasted and ground
3 Tbsp. Parmesan cheese
3 Tbsp. wheat germ or bread crumbs
1 unbaked 9-in. pie crust (see page 158)

Cut the broccoli flowerets into bite-sized pieces. Peel the thick stems and cut these into bite-sized pieces also. Place in a steamer over boiling water, and steam, covered, until just barely tender (4 to 5 minutes).

Sauté the onion in butter until golden, then add the flour and miso. Stir to blend, then add the water or stock and cook until thick. Remove from heat, and mix in tofu, Cheddar cheese, and sunflower seeds. Add steamed broccoli.

Toast sesame seeds by heating them in a cast iron skillet until they crackle. Grind toasted seeds in a blender, then mix them with the Parmesan cheese and wheat germ.

Pour the broccoli-tofu mixture into the unbaked pie crust, and top with the wheat germ mixture.

Bake at 425° for 15 minutes, then lower heat to 350° and bake 15 more minutes.

Let stand 10 minutes before serving.

Serves 6 to 8.

Variation: Omit pie crust. Bake in a 9 x 9-in. casserole at 350° for 30 minutes. Serve over bulgur wheat or brown rice.

VEGETABLE SHISHKABOBS

2 medium onions
2 bell peppers
2 dozen mushrooms with stems on
1 small eggplant
2 dozen baby onions
2 dozen cherry tomatoes
1 lb. tofu

½ cup vinegar
¾ cup red wine
2 Tbsp. tamari soy
2 cloves garlic, crushed
½ tsp. basil
½ tsp. oregano
1 cup olive oil

Start with the vegetables: Cut medium onions in eighths; seed bell peppers and cut in eighths. Clean mushrooms well and leave whole. Cut eggplant (unpeeled) in 1-in. cubes. Peel baby onions and leave whole. Remove stems from cherry tomatoes and wash. Cut tofu in 1-in. cubes.

Make the marinade by mixing all the remaining ingredients except the oil, then add the oil slowly, whisking constantly.

Add all the vegetables except the cherry tomatoes to the marinade, and allow to stand for at least 3 hours. Occasionally stir the marinade to be sure all the ingredients are evenly coated.

To prepare the shishkabobs, remove the vegetables and tofu from the marinade, and arrange on skewers. Add cherry tomatoes, and place bay leaves if desired between some of the vegetables.

Barbeque (or broil 3 in. from flame) until the tofu is lightly browned. Baste with extra marinade as they cook.

Serve on a bed of bulgur or rice.

Left-over marinade may be stored in a closed container in the refrigerator for later use.

Serves 4 to 6.

Desserts

PEANUT-RAISIN/
PEANUT-CAROB COOKIES

½ cup butter
¾ cup honey
½ cup peanut butter
1 egg

1 cup whole-wheat flour
1 tsp. salt
½ tsp. baking soda
½ tsp. baking powder

¼ cup milk
1 tsp. vanilla

3 cups rolled oats
1½ cups peanuts
1 cup raisins + 1 tsp. cinnamon,
    or 1 cup carob chips

Cream together the butter and the honey, then mix in the peanut butter and egg.

In a separate bowl, combine the flour, salt, baking soda, and baking powder.

Add the flour mixture to the butter mixture along with the milk and vanilla. Stir in the rolled oats and peanuts. Add the raisins or the carob chips.

Drop by spoonfuls on a greased cookie sheet, and bake at 325° for 15 minutes.

Makes 24 cookies.

WHOLE-WHEAT TEA COOKIES

These are crisp, light cookies, delicious by themselves, and irresistible when topped with Orange Cream Cheese (see below).

> 2 cups whole-wheat flour
> ½ cup wheat germ
> 1 tsp. baking powder
> ½ tsp. baking soda
> ¼ tsp. salt
>
> ½ cup butter
> ½ cup brown sugar or ⅓ cup honey
> ½ cup milk

Stir together the dry ingredients.

Cream the butter and brown sugar or honey, then add the flour mixture along with the milk, and mix well.

Roll the dough very thin on a floured board, then cut into circles, squares, or the shape of your fancy.

Place on an ungreased cookie sheet and bake at 350° for 12 to 15 minutes. The finished cookies should be crisp and light golden-brown.

Makes 4 dozen cookies.

ORANGE CREAM CHEESE

> ½ lb. cream cheese
> 1 tsp. lemon juice
> 2 tsp. honey
> juice of 1 orange (about ½ cup)
> 2 tsp. grated orange rind

Mix all of the ingredients together and chill. Serve with Tea Cookies and fruit.

Makes enough to frost 4 dozen cookies.

GRANOLA COOKIES

¼ cup soft butter or oil
¼ cup honey
2 Tbsp. molasses
1 tsp. vanilla

1¼ cups whole-wheat flour
1 tsp. baking soda

2 cups granola
½ cup raisins
¼ cup milk

Mix the liquid ingredients in one bowl, and the flour and soda in another. Add the dry to the liquid, and mix well.

Add the granola and the raisins, along with the milk, and blend thoroughly. (At this point, you might also add ½ cup of chopped dates if you really feel inspired.)

Drop by spoonfuls on a greased cookie sheet, and bake at 325° for 10 minutes.

Makes 24 cookies.

Note: These cookies are even better the second day, so try to save a few at least!

APPLESAUCE CAKE

½ cup butter
¾ cup honey
1 egg
1½ cups applesauce

1¾ cups whole-wheat pastry flour
¾ cup carob powder
1 tsp. nutmeg
1 tsp. cinnamon
½ tsp. cloves
½ tsp. salt
2 tsp. soda
½ cup raisins
½ cup walnuts, chopped

Cream together the butter and honey, then add the egg and applesauce and mix well.

In a separate bowl, mix the dry ingredients, including raisins and nuts.

Combine the wet and dry ingredients and mix well. Pour into a greased and floured 9 x 9-in. pan, and bake at 350° for 40 minutes.

Frost with cream cheese sweetened with honey if desired.

Serves 9.

MOLASSES CRUMB CAKE

3 Tbsp. butter or margarine
¾ cup boiling water
¾ cup molasses
1 tsp. baking soda

¾ cup dried whole-wheat
    bread crumbs
½ cup raisins
1 cup whole-wheat flour
¼ cup wheat germ
½ tsp. salt
2 tsp. ginger

Melt the butter by pouring the boiling water over it. Add the molasses and the soda.

In a separate bowl, mix together the remaining ingredients. Stir these into the molasses mixture, and pour into a greased and floured 9-in. round cake pan.

Bake at 325° for about 40 minutes, until a knife inserted into the center comes out clean.

Serves 8.

FRUIT PEMMICAN

This is a great backpacking or holiday treat!

> 1¼ cups pitted dates
> ⅔ cup raisins
> ⅓ cup dried apples
> ⅓ cup dried apricots
> ⅓ cup dried pineapple
> ⅓ cup sunflower seeds
> ½ cup cashews
>
> ½ cup peanut butter
> ⅓ cup carob powder

Finely grind dried fruits and nuts in a food grinder or processor. Add peanut butter and carob powder, mix thoroughly. Roll into balls, or mold into bars.
Yields 24 walnut-sized balls.

BANANA BONBONS

> 1 tsp. water
> 1 Tbsp. carob powder
> 2 tsp. honey
> 1 large ripe banana
> ¼ cup finely chopped almonds

Blend water, carob powder, and honey to make a paste. Cut banana into 8 pieces, about 1-in. lengths. Dip banana into carob mixture, then into chopped nuts.
Place on waxed paper on a plate, and freeze until firm.
Makes 8 bonbons.

FLAN

2 eggs
1¼ cups milk
1 Tbsp. light honey
1 tsp. vanilla
nutmeg

Beat the eggs, then add milk, honey, and vanilla, and blend well. Pour into four 6-oz. custard cups, and sprinkle with nutmeg.

Place custard cups in a baking dish with deep sides, and add hot water around the cups to ½-in. depth.

Bake at 350° for 40 minutes, or until knife inserted in center comes out clean.

Serves 4.

OKARA AND COCONUT MACAROONS

Okara is a by-product of the tofu-making process (see page 161). If you make tofu, these next two recipes are for you.

½ cup cream or evaporated milk
½ cup honey
2 cups shredded coconut
½ cup okara
¼ cup wheat germ
2 tsp. vanilla
¼ tsp. salt

Mix ingredients together well. Grease and flour a baking sheet, and drop mixture by tablespoon onto the sheet. Each cookie should be the size of a small walnut.

Bake at 350° for 10–15 minutes, or until lightly toasted.
Makes 3 dozen cookies.

OKARA TOFU SPICE BARS

⅓ cup okara
½ cup tofu
⅓ cup melted butter
½ cup honey
¼ cup molasses
1 cup applesauce or pumpkin pulp
½ cup buttermilk or ½ cup milk
  + 1½ tsp. vinegar

2½ cups whole-wheat flour
¼ cup wheat germ
1 tsp. baking powder
1 tsp. baking soda
½ tsp. salt
1½ tsp. cinnamon
½ tsp. ginger
½ tsp. nutmeg
¼ tsp. allspice
¼ tsp. cloves
¾ cup raisins
additional chopped dried fruits
  or nuts as desired

Combine okara, tofu, melted butter, honey, molasses, applesauce, and buttermilk in a blender and mix at high speed until mixture is very smooth.

Combine the remaining ingredients in a large bowl. Add the liquid ingredients, and stir to blend thoroughly.

Spoon batter into a greased and floured 8½ x 10½-in. baking dish, and bake at 350° for 40 minutes, or until the top springs back.

Cut into 20 2-in. squares.

YOGURT CHEESECAKE

This cheesecake is delicious plain, or with fruit on the top. It is *slightly* lower in calories than regular cheesecake because yogurt replaces some of the cream cheese.

> 2 cups crushed graham crackers
>   or granola (the granola
>   will produce a chewy crust)
> ¼ cup butter
> 2 Tbsp. honey
> ½ tsp. cinnamon (optional)
>
> 12 oz. softened cream cheese
> ¾ cup firm yogurt
> ¼ cup honey (light is best)
> 2 tsp. vanilla
> 1 Tbsp. lemon juice
> 2 tsp. grated lemon rind (optional)

To make the crust: Crush the crackers until they are quite fine. If you are using granola, you can leave it whole, or grind it in a food processor or blender.

Melt the butter and honey together. Mix with the crumbs, and press firmly into a 10-in. pie pan.

Bake in a 350° oven for 10 minutes. Cool.

For the filling: Beat all the remaining ingredients together until smooth and well blended. Spread into baked crust and chill 4 hours, until very cold.

TOFU CHEESECAKE

2 Tbsp. agar agar flakes*
¾ cup milk
½ cup honey
½ tsp. salt
4 tsp. grated lemon rind
4 Tbsp. lemon juice
2 tsp. vanilla
1½ lbs. fresh tofu
1 10-in. baked crumb crust (see page 149)
Lemon Glaze (see below)

Combine agar and milk, and let stand 5 minutes. Add honey and salt, and cook over low heat, stirring often, until mixture thickens slightly.

Pour milk mixture into a blender, add remaining ingredients, and blend until smooth.

Spread evenly into baked pie crust and chill for 1 hour. Top with Lemon Glaze, or other fruit topping, and chill at least 2 more hours.

LEMON GLAZE

3 Tbsp. cornstarch
¾ cup water
½ cup honey
¼ cup lemon juice
1 tsp. grated lemon rind

Combine cornstarch and water in a saucepan, and whisk smooth. Add remaining ingredients and heat gently until mixture thickens.

Allow to cool slightly, then spread over Tofu Cheese-cake.

Makes enough to cover 1 9-in.-round cake.

*Agar agar is a natural gelling agent, derived from seaweed. It can be purchased in most natural food stores and in Oriental markets. If you purchase it in an Oriental market, be sure to buy the white variety, rather than the pink which has been dyed.

VANILLA ICE CREAM

4 eggs
¾ cup light honey
1 qt. cream
2 cups milk
4½ tsp. vanilla

crushed ice
rock salt

Beat the eggs and honey together until the mixture is quite stiff. Fold in remaining ingredients, and pour into ice-cream freezer can (can should be no more than ¾ full). Place can in freezer.

Pack freezer with alternate layers of ice and salt, using the following proportions: after each 2 in. of ice, sprinkle on 3 Tbsp. of rock salt.

Place lid on freezer can and crank until ice cream is very firm (motor will stall on electric models). Add ice and salt as needed.

Makes about 1 gallon.

FROZEN YOGURT

4 cups fruit (strawberries,
*   peaches, bananas, etc.)*
1 quart yogurt
¾ cup honey (more or less to taste)
1 tsp. vanilla

Puree the fruit in a blender, or mash it well. Mix it with the remaining ingredients. Pour into ice-cream freezer and freeze as instructed. Remove dasher, recover, and pack with the recommended proportion of ice and salt. Let stand 1½ to 2 hours to ripen.

Makes one generous quart.

151

SIMPLE HONEY FROSTING

Try to find a light variety of honey, such as star thistle or clover, for making this frosting.

> ½ cup butter, softened
> ½ cup honey
> ½ cup dry milk powder
> 2 tsp. vanilla

Whip all ingredients together until light and fluffy.
  Makes slightly over 1 cup.

Cream Cheese Frosting:
Add ½ cup softened cream cheese to Simple Honey Frosting and whip until smooth.

Carob Frosting:
Add 2 Tbsp. carob powder to Simple Honey Frosting and beat until smooth and fluffy.

Lemon Frosting:
Add 2 Tbsp. lemon juice and 1 additional Tbsp. milk powder to Simple Honey Frosting or to Cream Cheese Frosting.

MIDDLE EASTERN BANANA
AND DATE DESSERT

4–5 large ripe bananas
½ lb. (about 2 cups) pitted dates
½ cup coarsely chopped
*   walnuts (optional)*
1–1½ cups heavy cream

In a serving dish, arrange alternate layers of thinly sliced bananas and halved dates. On top of each layer of dates, sprinkle a few of the walnuts (if you are using them).

Pour cream over all and chill several hours. The cream will soak into the fruit and give it a soft, slightly sticky texture—marvelous and rich!

Serves 6 to 8.

Variation: Follow above recipe, except layer dates and bananas in a baked, whole-wheat pie crust (see page 158).

Making the Basics

BASIC RICE RECIPE

2 cups water
¼–½ tsp. salt
1 cup brown rice

Add the salt to the water, and bring to a boil. Add rice, stirring just to mix. When water comes to boil again, reduce heat and cover. Simmer for 40 to 50 minutes.
Makes about 3 cups cooked rice.

Better-Than-Basic Rice:
Sauté rice in 1½ Tbsp. butter
before adding to boiling
water. Proceed as above.

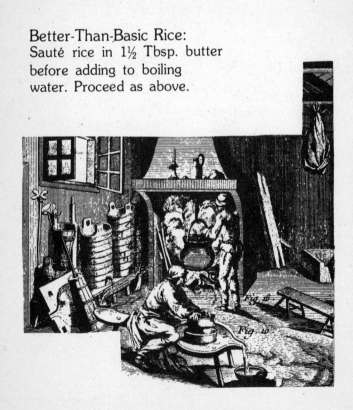

BULGUR WHEAT

Bulgur wheat is a whole wheat which has been cracked and lightly toasted. It is a delicious change of pace from rice, and cooks in about half the time. Below are two basic methods for cooking bulgur wheat.

I: 2 cups water
    ¼ tsp. salt
    1 cup bulgur

Bring the water to a boil, then add the salt and the bulgur. Stir just to mix. When the water comes to a boil again, reduce heat and cover. Simmer for 20 minutes.

II: 1 Tbsp. butter
     1 cup bulgur
     ¼ tsp. salt
     2 cups boiling water

Melt the butter and add the bulgur. Cook over medium heat for 2 to 3 minutes, stirring often.

Add the salt and the boiling water. Allow the water to come to a boil once again, then reduce the heat and cover. Simmer for about 20 minutes.

Both methods make about 2½ cups cooked bulgur.

WHOLE-WHEAT EGG NOODLES

2 egg yolks
1 whole egg
2 Tbsp. water
1 tsp. olive oil
½ tsp. salt
¼ cup wheat germ
1¼ cups whole-wheat flour
Additional whole-wheat flour
for kneading and rolling

In a small bowl, lightly beat together egg yolks, egg, water, and oil.

In a larger bowl, combine salt, wheat germ, and 1¼ cups flour; make a well in the center.

Pour egg mixture into flour well and mix with a fork. Gather dough into a ball.

Knead on a floured board until very smooth, about 4 minutes if you are planning to use a pasta machine, about 10 if you are going to roll it by hand.

To roll and cut with a pasta machine: After kneading 4 minutes by hand, divide dough into fourths. Slightly flatten one portion of dough; cover the remainder. Feed dough through the smooth rollers, set as far apart as possible. Refold into thirds and feed through again; repeat folding and rolling 5 or 6 more times. If dough is sticky, flour both sides each time you roll.

Set rollers one notch closer together and feed dough through (without folding) 2 or 3 more times. Cut length in half so dough is easier to handle. Repeat rolling, setting rollers closer each time. Feed dough through each setting 1 or 2 times until it's ¹⁄₁₅-in. thick (on most machines, this is the third from last notch).

Put desired cutting blade on machine; feed dough through. Lay noodles slightly apart on waxed paper or cloth towels. Let dry until all are rolled and cut.

Cook immediately (this takes just a few minutes), or wrap well to store. Refrigerate up to 2 days or freeze up to 1 month.

To roll and cut by hand: After kneading 10 minutes by

hand, divide dough into fourths. On a floured board, roll 1 portion of dough (cover remainder) into a rectangle about 5-in. wide and 1/16-in. thick. If dough is sticky, turn and flour both sides as you roll. Cut into desired shapes and set on waxed paper or cloth towels. Let dry until all dough is rolled.

Makes about ¾ lb. noodles.

WHOLE-WHEAT PIE CRUST

> 1½ cups whole-wheat pastry flour
> ½ cup wheat germ
> ½ tsp. salt
> ½ cup butter or shortening
> 4–6 Tbsp. cold water

Stir together dry ingredients, then cut in the butter. When the mixture is the consistency of coarse cornmeal, add the water and mix just until the dough holds together.

Form into two balls, flatten, and roll out on a lightly floured surface until large enough to fit a 9-in. pie plate. Then, starting at the outer edge, roll the dough up loosely around the rolling pin, and unroll it into the pie plate.

For a baked crust: Bake at 400° for 10 minutes.

For an unbaked crust: Fill and bake as directed.

Makes 2 9-in. pie crusts.

YOGURT

There are as many ways to make yogurt as there are people who make it. The recipe that follows is the one that has worked best for me.

The only equipment you really need (and I suppose you could even manage without this) is a cooking thermometer (or any thermometer which will register 160° and 108°).

I use a yogurt maker (an $8 model) because I like the security of knowing my yogurt will work.

You will notice that the recipe calls for low-fat milk. It seems that a bit of fat is necessary in order for the yogurt to set up. Of course you could use whole milk, but why add the extra fat and calories?

> 4 cups low-fat milk
> ⅓ cup non-instant milk powder
> 1 Tbsp. plain yogurt
>
> cooking thermometer

Blend milk and milk powder until no longer lumpy.

Place the milk mixture in a pan and heat to scalding (160°): this is the point when a lot of steam will begin rising off the milk.

Allow the milk to cool to 108°, or until it no longer feels hot when a few drops are placed on your wrist. (It is a good idea to keep the milk covered with a dish towel or loose lid while it is cooling, to keep dust and spores in the air from falling into it.)

Add the cooled milk slowly to the 1 Tbsp. yogurt.

Stir to mix thoroughly, then incubate one of the following ways: in a commercial yogurt maker, in a covered container in an oven with a pilot light, or in any other place that maintains a temperature of about 110°.

Let stand about 6 hours, undisturbed, then check the consistency. If it is still too runny, let it set a bit longer. It should be noted that the longer you let it set, the firmer and *tarter* it will become. It should also be noted that homemade yogurt never seems to get quite as thick as the commercial varieties (they often cheat, using gelatin, bean gum, and other thickeners).

If you use your own yogurt for starter, you may find that it begins to lose its potency in time (i.e., yogurt no longer gets firm). When this happens, buy a small carton of commercial yogurt and start fresh. When you buy yogurt for starter, that made without additional thickeners (gelatin, bean gum, etc.) seems to work best.

If your yogurt does not thicken, use it for cooking: bread, pancakes, soup, etc.

Add fruit and sweeteners, if desired, after yogurt has thickened.

Makes 1 qt.

BUTTERMILK

3½ cups nonfat milk
½ cup buttermilk

Heat milk to scalding (160°).

Cool to 100°, then add it slowly to buttermilk.

When the milk and the buttermilk are well blended, pour into a quart jar. Wrap well in 2 to 3 towels and place in a warm spot (at least 78°) for 24 hours, or until thick.

Chill thoroughly, and enjoy the thickest, tangiest buttermilk you've ever had!

Makes 1 qt.

MAKING TOFU

Homemade tofu is not difficult to make; it just takes time. The finished product is well worth it, however, as it is much milder in flavor than that available commercially. Homemade tofu is also very inexpensive: 25¢ a pound, which is quite a bargain when you consider that it is equivalent to beef in its protein content.

> 1½ cups dry soybeans
> 6½ cups water
> 8 cups boiling water
> ¾ cup nigari (purchase at
>   health food store or
>   Oriental market)
>
> cheesecloth (2 pieces at least
>   30 x 30-in.)
> colander
> large heavy kettle
> blender or food grinder

Wash soybeans several times, then soak in water for 10 hours (makes 4 cups soaked).

Rinse soaked beans thoroughly.

Place 1 cup soaked beans into blender, add 1½ cups boiling water, and blend thoroughly. Pour into cheese-cloth-lined colander.

Blend 2 more cups beans, as above, and pour into cheesecloth.

Twist cheesecloth and press with a spoon to expel all the soy milk. Return the pulp to the blender, add 2 cups boiling water, and blend to mix. Pour into cheesecloth and drain as before to remove all soy milk. Set the pulp (okara) aside.

Process remaining beans as above.

When all the soybeans are done, pour the soy milk into a heavy kettle and bring to a boil over medium heat, *stirring constantly.* (An alternative is to heat it in your crock pot over high heat; this takes about 3 hours—no stirring, no sticking.)

Let the soy milk boil for 10 minutes. During this time,

dissolve ¾ tsp. nigari in ½ cup water. When the milk has boiled for 10 minutes, pour the nigari mixture into it gradually, stirring gently (so as not to break the curds). Stir 5 or 6 times, then hold the spoon upright and motionless to ensure thorough distribution of the nigari.

Allow to sit 5 minutes, or until curds are formed and the whey is a brown color rather than milky. Ladle curds into a cheesecloth-lined colander, gently so as not to break the curds, and allow to sit 5 minutes.

For hard tofu, gather edges of cheesecloth and hang for 10 to 40 minutes.

Remove pressed curds and store in closed container or in water in refrigerator.

Makes 1 lb. tofu.

ZUCCHINI RELISH

This can be used in place of pickle relish, and is a great way to use lots of zucchini.

> 12 cups ground zucchini
> 9 cups finely chopped onion
> 4 cups ground bell pepper
> 2 tsp. turmeric
> 1 Tbsp. celery seed
> 1 tsp. dry mustard
> 2 tsp. mustard seed
> 4 cups vinegar
> 3 cups honey

Grind the vegetables in a food grinder or processor. Combine with remaining ingredients and simmer for 20 minutes, until vegetables are tender but still crisp.

Pack hot into hot, sterilized jars to within ½ in. of top. Process in boiling water for 20 minutes.

Makes about 10 pints.

BASIC TOMATO SAUCE

2 Tbsp. olive oil
1 small onion, chopped
2 cloves garlic, minced
1 carrot, grated
1 small bell pepper, chopped
1 bay leaf
1 tsp. basil
1 tsp. oregano

½ tsp. thyme
2 Tbsp. chopped parsley
½ tsp. salt
1 28-oz. can tomatoes,
   chopped, with liquid
1 6-oz. can tomato paste
¼ cup red wine (optional)

In a large pan, sauté the onion until it is golden. Add the remaining ingredients and simmer for 30 minutes.
   Remove bay leaf.
   Makes about 3 cups.

TOMATO CATSUP

12 cups chopped fresh tomatoes
   or
2 28-oz. cans whole tomatoes
   and 1 15-oz. can tomato sauce

2 onions, chopped
1 bell pepper, chopped
½ cup apple cider vinegar

½ cup honey
½ tsp. allspice
¼ tsp. cinnamon
⅛ tsp. dry mustard
⅛ tsp. garlic powder
⅛ tsp. cloves
⅛ tsp. celery seed
pinch cayenne

Combine all ingredients and simmer over low heat, or in a crock pot, until the volume is halved. Cool.
   Pour into blender, and blend until totally smooth. Pour into bottles.
   This catsup can be canned, frozen, or kept in the refrigerator for about 3 months.
   Makes about 2½ pints.

APPLESAUCE

> *about 16 apples (Pippins or*
>   *combined green varieties)*
> *½–1 cup water*
> *cinnamon and cloves (optional)*

Slice and core apples.

Place in a large kettle or crock pot with ½ cup water, and simmer over *low* heat until the apples are tender. During this time, the pot should be covered, and you should check the apples occasionally to make sure there is still liquid on the bottom. If the bottom of the pot gets dry, add an additional ½ cup water.

When the apples are tender, put them through a sieve or ricer (or comparable food grinder), or you can leave them in chunks.

Add cinnamon and cloves to taste if desired, and serve warm or cold.

Serves 8.

Note: If you like a tarter applesauce, or if your apples are especially bland, you can add 1–2 Tbsp. lemon juice.

BAKING POWDER

2 Tbsp. baking soda
2 Tbsp. cream of tartar
2 Tbsp. cornstarch or
    arrowroot powder

Sift all ingredients together 3 times; store in an airtight container.

CURRY POWDER

9 tsp. ground coriander seed
7 tsp. turmeric
2½ tsp. cumin
2½ tsp. ground fenugreek seed
1 tsp. dry mustard
1 tsp. allspice
1 tsp. red pepper
½ tsp. ginger
¼ tsp. cloves
¼ tsp. cinnamon
⅛ tsp. cayenne

Sift all ingredients together 2 or 3 times. Store in an airtight container.

CHILI POWDER

7 Tbsp. red pepper
2½ tsp. cumin
1 tsp. oregano
½ tsp. salt
½ tsp. garlic powder

Sift all ingredients together 2 or 3 times. Store in an airtight container.

Substitutions
and Equivalents

SUBSTITUTIONS

INGREDIENTS

For:	Use:
1 tsp. baking powder	½ tsp. soda + ½ tsp. cream of tartar
	or ½ tsp. soda + 1½ tsp. lemon juice or vinegar
	or ½ tsp. soda + ½ cup sour milk or buttermilk in place of ½ cup milk in recipe
1 Tbsp. cornstarch	2 tsp. arrowroot
	or 2 Tbsp. flour
2 Tbsp. tapioca	3 Tbsp. flour
2 egg yolks	1 whole egg
1 cup milk	¼ cup milk powder + 1 cup water
	or ½ cup evaporated milk + ½ cup water
1 cup sour milk	1 cup buttermilk
	or 1 cup yogurt
	or 1 Tbsp. vinegar or lemon juice + milk to make 1 cup
1 cup sour cream	½ cup yogurt + ½ cup cottage cheese, blended
1 tsp. dried herbs	1 Tbsp. fresh herbs

BAKING PAN SUBSTITUTIONS

For:	Use:
Round pans:	
Two 8-in. round	Two 8 × 8-in. square
Two 9-in. round	Two 8 × 8-in. square
	or three 8-in. round
Square pans:	
one 8 × 8-in square	one 9-in. round
one 9 × 9-in. square	two 8-in. round
two 8 × 8-in. square	two 9-in. round
	or one 9 × 13-in. rectangle
two 9 × 9-in. square	three 8-in. round
Rectangular pans:	
one 8 × 12-in.	two 8-in. round
one 9 × 13-in.	two 9-in. round
	or two 8 × 8-in. square
Loaf pans:	
one 4 × 8-in. loaf	one 8 × 8-in. square
one 5 × 9-in. loaf	one 9 × 9-in. square
Tube pans:	
one 9 × 3½-in. tube	two 9-in. layers
one 10 × 4-in. tube	two 5 × 9-in. loaf
	or one 9 × 13-in. rectangle

EQUIVALENTS

		Weight	Approximate Measure
Dairy products	butter/margarine	1 lb.	2 cups
	cheese	1 lb.	5 cups, grated
	cottage cheese	1 lb.	2 cups
	dry milk powder	1 lb.	4 cups
Dried beans	black beans	1 lb.	2 cups
	black-eyed peas	1 lb.	2½ cups
	garbanzos	1 lb.	2¼ cups
	kidney beans	1 lb.	2¼ cups
	lentils	1 lb.	2¼ cups
	lima beans	1 lb.	2 cups
	navy beans	1 lb.	2 cups
	pinto beans	1 lb.	2½ cups
	soybeans	1 lb.	2½ cups
	split peas	1 lb.	2 cups
Eggs	6 medium		1 cup
Flours	cornmeal	1 lb.	4 cups
	soy flour	1 lb.	4 cups
	unbleached	1 lb.	4 cups
	whole-wheat	1 lb.	4 cups
	buckwheat	1 lb.	2½ cups
Grains	bulgur wheat	1 lb.	2¾ cups
	millet	1 lb.	2 cups
	pasta	1 lb.	5 cups dry (approx.)
	pasta	1 lb.	8–10 cups cooked
	rice, brown	1 lb.	2 cups
	rolled oats	1 lb.	4 cups

		Weight	Approximate Measure
Fruits and vegetables	apples	1 lb.	4 medium whole
		1 lb.	4 cups, sliced
	bananas	1 lb.	4 medium
		1 lb.	2 cups mashed
	carrots	1 lb.	4 medium
	celery	1 lb.	6–7 stalks
	mushrooms	1 lb.	5 cups, sliced
	onions	1 lb.	2–3 medium
	potatoes	1 lb.	3–4 medium
		1 lb.	2 cups mashed
	tomatoes	1 lb.	4–5 medium
Nuts and seeds	almonds	1 lb. shelled	3 cups
		1 lb. unshelled	1½ cups shelled
	coconut	1 lb.	5 cups
	peanuts*	1 lb.	2½ cups
	peanut butter*	1 lb.	1½ cups
	sunflower seeds	1 lb.	4 cups
	walnuts	1 lb. shelled	4 cups
		1 lb. unshelled	1½ cups shelled
Sweeteners	date sugar	1 lb.	3 cups
	honey	1 lb.	1¾ cups
	molasses	1 lb.	1¾ cups
	sugar, brown	1 lb.	2¼ cups

*Peanuts are actually legumes.

EQUIVALENT MEASURES

pinch	=	less than ⅛ teaspoon
3 teaspoons	=	1 tablespoon
2 tablespoons	=	1 ounce
4 tablespoons	=	¼ cup (2 ounces)
16 tablespoons	=	1 cup (8 ounces)
2 cups	=	1 pint (16 ounces)
4 cups	=	1 quart
4 quarts	=	1 gallon

COMMERCIAL CAN SIZES

Can size	Weight	Approximate cups
6 oz. (tomato paste)	6 oz.	¾ cup
8 oz.	8 oz.	1 cup
No. 1 or picnic	10½ oz.	1¼ cups
No. 300	15½ oz.	1¾ cups
No. 303	16 oz. (1 lb.)	2 cups
No. 2	1 lb., 4 oz.	2½ cups
No. 2½ (whole tomatoes)	1 lb., 12 oz.	3½ cups
46 oz. (fruit juices)	46 oz.	5¾ cups

Sources

Here is a list—by no means exhaustive—of additional sources of information on vegetarian cooking.

The Book of Tofu, by William Shurtleff and Akiko Aoyagi. This is a beautiful book about one of the most economical and healthful protein foods available: tofu. It contains a clear description of how to make tofu, and about 500 recipes for using it. Autumn Press, large-size paperback, $7.95; Bantam Books, small paperback, $2.95.

Diet for a Small Planet, by Frances Moore Lappe. This book contains a good summary of the reasons for being a vegetarian. There is a fairly good description of protein and protein complementarity, and some extremely helpful charts. There are a number of recipes, some of which are good, and some which leave a lot to be desired, tastewise. Ballantine Books, spiral bound, $6.95; paperback, $2.50.

Laurel's Kitchen, by Laurel Robertson, Carol Flinders, and Bronwen Godfrey. This is my very favorite vegetarian cookbook. It is a beautiful all-around book. It contains an excellent discussion of the reasons for being vegetarian, with an emphasis on the world food situation. It has an excellent section on nutrition, good for vegetarian and nonvegetarian alike. The authors try very hard to keep dairy products, eggs, sugar, and salt to a minimum. Most of the recipes are fairly easy to prepare, and are delicious. Nilgiri Press, hardcover, $15; Bantam Books, paperback, $3.95.

Moosewood Cookbook, by Mollie Katzen. This is an excellent vegetarian cookbook by a woman who is a cook at the Moosewood Restaurant (hence the name of the book) in Ithaca, New York. The recipes are superb, and not overly difficult to prepare; required preparation times are given for each recipe. There is a good variety of recipes, and use of sugar and white flour is minimal. Highly

173

recommended. Ten Speed Press, hardcover, $9.95; paperback, $7.95.

Recipes for a Small Planet, by Ellen Buchman Ewald. This book contains a brief discussion of protein, and many recipes with good amino acid combinations. Some of the recipes are quite good, and some seem to sacrifice taste for protein. Ballantine Books, spiral bound, $6.95; paperback, $2.50.

Stocking Up, by Carol H. Stoner. Although this is not a vegetarian cookbook per se, it is an excellent reference source for persons wishing to preserve their own food. It tells how to preserve all types of foods naturally. It covers harvesting, canning, freezing, and drying of fruits and vegetables. It also discusses storing and freezing of dairy products, and making cheese, butter, and yogurt. Honey is used as a sweetener in the recipes. Rodale Press, hardcover, $12.95.

Tassajara Cooking, by Edward Espe Brown. This is the ideal book for the creative cook. The author suggests various ingredients for each recipe, but the actual ingredients and amounts are left up to you. Shambhala Publications, paperback, $5.95.

The Vegetarian Alternative, by Victor Sussman. This book presents an excellent general discussion of vegetarianism, without being preachy. The explanation of protein and protein complementarity is clear and easy to follow. There are a few recipes in the back of the book, but it is not really a cookbook. Rodale Press, paperback, $6.95.

The Vegetarian Epicure I and *The Vegetarian Epicure II,* by Anna Thomas. These books both contain excellent gourmet recipes that will impress even your most uppity friends. Many of the recipes are quite rich (they do call for sugar, white flour, cream, and lots of butter), but they are always delicious. Most of the recipes are fairly time-consuming to prepare, but worth the time if you love really fine food. Alfred A. Knopf, *I,* $5.95; *II,* $6.95.

INDEX